Paranormal Illinois

Michael Kleen

Schiffer Publishing Ltd

4880 Lower Valley Road Atglen, Pennsylvania 19310

Schiffer Books are available at special discounts for bulk purchases for sales promotions or premiums. Special editions, including personalized covers, corporate imprints, and excerpts can be created in large quantities for special needs. For more information contact the publisher:

Published by Schiffer Publishing Ltd.
4880 Lower Valley Road
Atglen, PA 19310
Phone: (610) 593-1777; Fax: (610) 593-2002
E-mail: Info@schifferbooks.com

For the largest selection of fine reference books on this and related subjects,
please visit our web site at **www.schifferbooks.com**
We are always looking for people to write books on new and related subjects.
If you have an idea for a book please contact us at the above address.

This book may be purchased
from the publisher.
Include $5.00 for shipping.
Please try your bookstore first.
You may write for a free catalog.

In Europe, Schiffer books are distributed by:
Bushwood Books
6 Marksbury Ave.
Kew Gardens
Surrey TW9 4JF England
Phone: 44 (0) 20 8392-8585;
Fax: 44 (0) 20 8392-9876
E-mail: info@bushwoodbooks.co.uk
Website: www.bushwoodbooks.co.uk

Text and photos by Michael Kleen
Copyright © 2010 by Michael Kleen
Library of Congress Control Number: 2009939148

Designed by RoS
Type set in Rosemary Roman/New Baskerville BT

ISBN: 978-0-7643-3430-6

Printed in The United States of America

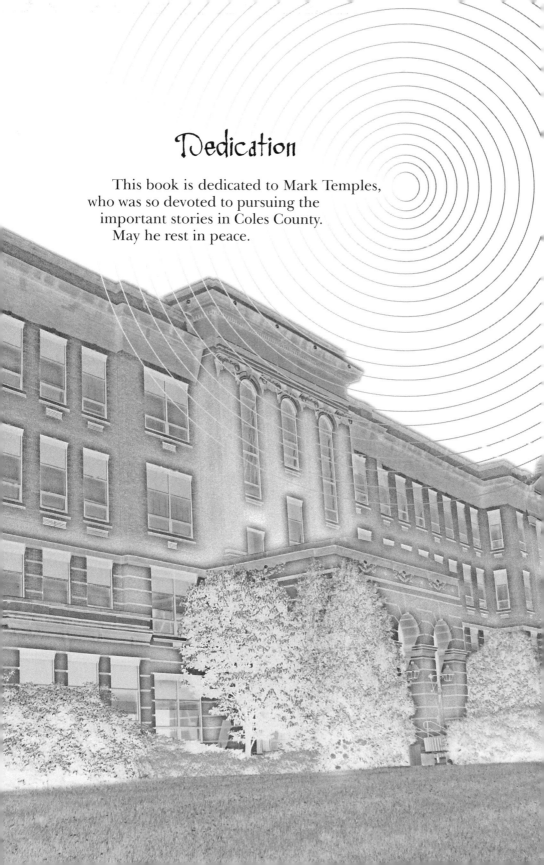

Dedication

This book is dedicated to Mark Temples,
who was so devoted to pursuing the
important stories in Coles County.
May he rest in peace.

Contents

Introduction

What are Folk Stories and Legends?

The American Heritage Dictionary of the English Language defines a legend as an unverified story handed down from earlier times, or a romanticized or popularized myth of modern times. It defines folklore as the traditional beliefs, myths, tales, and practices of a people, transmitted orally, or a popular but unfounded belief. These two categories encompass a broad range of stories. Sometimes these stories are a somewhat-vivid memory of an event long ago, or sometimes they are murky, highly fictional accounts of recent events. Folklore and legends are continuously created in college dorm rooms, high school hallways, bedrooms, bars, tour buses, libraries, the World Wide Web—anywhere we freely communicate. Today's event, over time, becomes tomorrow's legend. What seems like something completely mundane to us now, or so horrifying that we would want to quickly forget about it, occasionally crops up years or decades later, often in a form that we might not expect or even recognize.

This book primarily delves into the ghostlore of Illinois. Ghostlore is a subcategory of folklore that deals with—you guessed it—stories regarding hauntings or spirits of the dead. Of course, in order for there to be a ghost, someone somewhere had to have died. Therefore, a death, whether real or imagined, precipitates the majority of these legends: the discovery of a lifeless body, drownings, suicides, murders, and even the metaphorical death of institutions like mental hospitals and old schoolhouses. Since those events are a part of local history, they are frequently the well from which the elements of these stories are drawn.

When we look at local history from that angle we can see why folklore and ghost stories have such an intimate relationship. Local history, I believe, is usually divided into three different consciousnesses. There is the surface consciousness of current events, where the interesting stories of the day are ingested and then forgotten; the historical consciousness, where events like the foundation of a city or who was mayor in 1930 are cleaned up and simplified for public sentiment; and the folk-consciousness, where the darker aspects of history are related from a "safe" distance. No one wants to teach their children that the town in which they live is soaked in the blood of past and present generations. We want to teach them the *Barney and Friends* version of history, so we leave it to them to uncover and reinvent the more unpleasant aspects of the past through folklore, legends, and ghost stories.

Does that mean folklore arises from the suppression of negative events? In one sense, yes, but it is not that Illinois is an unusually dangerous place masquerading as a safe one. The pain, frustration, anger, and fear that accompanies a murder or suicide, or even thoughts of death in general, are feelings that most people would not want to revisit every waking moment. Still, to forget about an unpleasant event does a disservice not only to the memories of the people involved, but also can create a distorted sense of reality. In some cases, forgetting the specific nature of a crime or calamity leads people to blow the incident out of proportion, or to invent details where none were before. At that point, fear replaces facts about a specific event with urban legends and folklore. For instance, when James Dallas Egbert III disappeared into the steam tunnels under Michigan State University in 1979 with a bottle of sedatives intent on ending his life, he inadvertently created a legend known as the "Steam Tunnel Incident." A private investigator named William Dear concocted a theory, based on inaccurate information, that James had gotten lost in the steam tunnels while attempting to play a live action version of the game Dungeons & Dragons. Even though Dear's theory was nonsense, James' college peers disregarded the truth of the matter and started telling stories about role players being found dead in underground steam tunnels. Over time, the legend became the "truth," and most people forgot about poor James Egbert.

As demonstrated by the case of the university steam tunnels, folklore serves its purpose by providing people with a template for why they should be wary of a particular place or situation. Remembering that a local girl was found murdered near a creek on September 23, 1976, for instance, is too intellectually burdensome, but "the white lady of Briar Creek" provides a colorful story that distances people from the event while still providing a potent, continuous reminder free from the inconvenience of specific facts.

Most importantly, human beings love a good story. We prefer dream images to those of reality, and the wilder the story the better. So while reinforcing our own sense of fear and paranoia, why not make it entertaining as well? For example, in the instance of the legend of "Devil's Gate," it was not enough for local residents that a playground of abandoned buildings opened up during the 1990s. There had to have been murders. Not only were there murders, the curious imagined, but these murders took place at a girl's school at the hands of a deranged janitor or escaped lunatic. Then, since that apparently wasn't interesting enough, the murderer had to decapitate the girls and hang their heads on the spikes of the gate, and so on. At first, no one familiar with the area really believes these grossly embellished details, yet the storytellers aren't harangued for being liars. This is because most listeners are willing to suspend their knowledge of reality for the sake of entertainment. Unfortunately, after a while hardly anyone gives consideration to the real events behind the stories.

Is it right to invent stories about something so terrible as murder or suicide? While some are strictly fictional, the origins of many tales in this book *did* involve the death of a real person, and when telling the history of deaths of any kind, it is important to always remember that the totality of a given person is not in the final moments of his or her life. But the unfortunate reality is that, like politicians and celebrities, a victim of murder suddenly becomes a public interest even if he or she lived his or her entire life in obscurity. Yet we should not delude ourselves. Even if the act of relating stories of death for public consumption makes us ethically uncomfortable, the morbid curiosity of the public is unquenchable. It is a guilty pleasure that led kids in Los Gatos, California to repeatedly visit a boy's discarded corpse for fifteen years before the authorities found out and did anything about it (the bones were subsequently lost in a police warehouse and never buried). But it is a pleasure that can only be safely indulged if the person of interest remains anonymous or distant. As long as the murdered Jane Doe is just an abstract character and not your own wife or daughter the story is fascinating instead of terrible. Because of this distance, and the lack of access to firsthand information that accompanies it, those of us not close to the actual event frequently invent facts and explanations to fill in the blanks. Those inventions are then passed on from one person to the next, until they become abstract and take on a life of their own.

Thusly, folklore becomes intimately connected with the tragic and macabre as a way of transmitting information about unfortunate events far beyond the actual events themselves. Inevitably, a new generation grows up and stories involving strange noises, sightings, and phantoms surround the location of the tragedy; although, unless it had been particularly well known, most people cannot recall why the location is so terrifying beyond the ghost stories themselves. After a long period of time (apparently ten or fifteen years will suffice under the right conditions) the stories become so convoluted that people actually begin to believe a killer hung heads from the gates of St. Francis Boy's Camp, or that a headless horseman stalks the banks of LaKey Creek. But many times, it is not necessary for anything extraordinary to have happened at all. An abandoned building and a few unanswered questions are enough to get most people's imagination racing.

Are These Stories True?

The stories in this book are based on real places and events, but may contain a large dose of imaginative creativity. At all times, I have made an effort to thoroughly document any and all sources, and to distinguish hard facts from the folklore. Since legends and folklore are usually based on events that are left out of the historical narrative, getting to the facts behind them is extremely difficult. Personal testimonials are all but useless when it comes to an objective account, and even newspaper articles are sometimes more rumor mill than record. But because the everyday workings of these locations do not warrant newspaper articles or much mention in history books, there are large gaps in the facts pertaining to places like Airtight Bridge and Maple Lake. The records have been lost because no one thought they would be historically important, so only the stories remain.

Irreparably complicating matters, time distorts what was at one point common knowledge. For example, in the legend of Lakey's Creek, the family of Simon Leakey knew the circumstances surrounding his murder, but because no one thought those details were important enough to write down, there are no firsthand accounts to prove or disprove the stories we hear today. No matter how much research is done, no one will ever know what happened. The best we can do is piece together a story and borrow from our general knowledge of similar events or circumstances that we do know more about. Faced with this situation, we should report the facts as we find them, interpret their cultural context in regards to what was *most likely* the case, and consider everything else to be false but not irrelevant.

Our analysis so far leaves us with the realization that legends and folklore are often more fiction than fact. So why are books of folklore considered to be factual? Is there a difference between a historical novel and a book of folklore? They are both stories based on historical places or events. Facts about the battle of Gettysburg are readily available, yet Michael Shaara's *The Killer Angels* is recognized as a work of fiction while Troy Taylor's *Haunted Illinois* is considered nonfiction.

Presentation is the obvious difference between the two. A historical fiction novel is presented as fiction based on fact, while a book of folklore is presented as factual in terms of the fact that people have told those stories about a certain location, while leaving it up to the reader to determine if the content of the individual stories themselves are true. But isn't there some deception inherent in that? If someone claims to see a ghost in a cemetery late at night, is that somehow more credible than someone who just makes up a story about seeing a ghost in the cemetery late at night? If the person is a good liar, how can we tell the difference? How do we know they just don't really want to see their name in a book or newspaper? People have gone to much more extremes to get attention.

Depending on their worldview, readers of folklore will look at its truthfulness in different ways. If your worldview includes a belief in ghosts, then hearing a local legend about a ghost, or eyewitness accounts of ghosts, will confirm your belief. If your worldview excludes ghosts from the realm of the possible, then any claims of ghosts will be dismissed as fantasy. So whether a book of folklore is considered factual or not depends on the reader's beliefs. Of course, short of an admission by the storyteller or a debunking through our own rational analysis, we will never know if the stories told are true or not. Therefore, like other books of folklore, I am leaving it up to the reader to decide whether or not the stories in this book are true.

Are You a Paranormal Investigator?

I am not a paranormal investigator, and this book has nothing whatsoever to do with applying science (or pseudo-science) to stories of the paranormal. I am a local historian, a folklorist, a story teller, a publisher, a music lover, a dabbler in philosophy, but I am not a paranormal investigator and I do not claim to be a scientist. Although I have devoted long hours and many, many years to collecting ghost stories, the paranormal has never been more than an interest for me.

I recommend *The Last Laugh* by Dr. Raymond Moody to all my readers obsessed with finding "the truth" behind every ghost story. In *The Last Laugh*, Dr. Moody argued that three groups of people entrenched in their perspectives on the paranormal—parapsychologists, professional skeptics, and Christian fundamentalists—have been batting around the same arguments for over a century. None of these groups have conclusively proven their case nor advanced the study of the subject any farther. In the end, he believes, it is the people who enjoy the paranormal on its own terms that come the closest to learning anything about it. I urge all of my readers to take Dr. Moody's prescription and lighten up about this particular subject. After all, until we discover the ultimate truths of the universe (we've been trying for thousands of years) we will never know if such a thing as a ghost even exists. Furthermore, we have no way of knowing whether such a thing as a ghost can even be measured by mechanical instruments, or exposed through experimental science.

Eminent men, such as Edmund Gurney, William Jones, Alfred Russel Wallace (co-discoverer of natural selection), and Harry Houdini, have tried for centuries to uncover the truth behind the paranormal, and so far, all their efforts have failed to produce anything resembling conclusive proof. Perhaps some things were never meant to be understood. Perhaps understanding absolutely everything would destroy what makes life remotely interesting. Maybe there is nothing to find. I don't know. I don't have the answers to these questions, and I would be a fool if I pretended that I did. But we can choose to approach these questions intelligently by studying science, philosophy, history, theology and other subjects that investigate human experience, or we can sit in front of the television or behind computer screens and blindly believe everything that is presented. Dr. Moody's greatest insight was that the paranormal is entertainment. It would seem rather silly for someone to take a thermometer into a funhouse in order to "prove or disprove" the attraction!

So join me as we have fun with the paranormal in our great state of Illinois. Suspend your disbelief as you examine the history of our local ghostlore at one of the nearly two dozen locations presented in this book. I dare you to put down the EMF detector—or your wall of skepticism—and pick up your imagination. You might be surprised at what you rediscover.

Part 1
Archer Avenue

CEMETERY NOT
RESPONSIBLE
FOR ACCIDENTS
OR INJURIES TO
VISITORS OR
THEIR PROPERTY

CEMETERY
HOURS

ARCHER WOODS

FELIX
NO. 25. C. F. D.
COMPLEMENTS OF
E. WUNDERLICH GRANITE CO.

Archer Avenue and the Enigma of Chicago's Southwest Suburban "Triangle"

Archer Avenue begins near Chinatown at S. State Street in Chicago and travels steadily west until merging with Route 171 in suburban Summit. There the road turns sharply southwest at an obtuse angle, then runs parallel with the Chicago Sanitary and Ship Canal. It passes through Justice and Willow Springs before ultimately entering scenic Lemont. It is near these three villages—Justice, Willow Springs, and Lemont—where the road has gained an unusual reputation. Starting with Resurrection Cemetery and ending at St. James-Sag Church, this section of Archer Avenue forms the northern border of a triangle of forest preserves, lakes, trails, and burial grounds that could easily be described as Chicago's backyard.

Encompassing most of the Cook County Forest Preserve District's Palos Division, this triangle is defined by the Calumet Sag Channel to the south, Archer Avenue and the Des Plaines River to the north, and S. Kean Avenue to the west. It is a hilly, wooded area filled with over a dozen small lakes and sloughs—shallow depressions that often fill with water during the spring and summer. At the hinterlands of civilization, this area has a well-deserved reputation built upon generations of strange encounters and creative storytelling. It is home to no less than ten mystery sites involving everything from hauntings, to unsolved murders, to healing springs, to the site of America's second nuclear reactor. These locations dot the area on either side of Archer Avenue, with the majority falling inside the boundaries of the triangle.

The unusual qualities of this southwest suburban wilderness make it a favorite for ghost tours, paranormal researchers, and curiosity seekers alike, not to mention hikers, horseback riders, fishermen, and the many thousands who come there to escape from the hustle and bustle of the big city, if only for an afternoon. The roads there are long and dark, the lakes and parks remote, and the landmarks emerge from the shadows to capture the imagination of visitors.

There are five locations in and around this area that are well known to locals and obligatory inclusions in the annals of ghostlore: Resurrection Cemetery and the famous hitchhiking specter of Resurrection Mary, Archer Woods Cemetery, Maple Lake, St. James-Sag Church and

Cemetery, and German Church Road—the road along which motorists discovered the bodies of the Grimes sisters in 1957. In addition to these heavyweights, there are at least seven lesser known locations in the vicinity with equally strange and fascinating stories: Bethania Cemetery, the Why Not drive-in, the Justice Public Library, Healing Waters Park, Fairmount Hills Cemetery, the intersection of 95th and Kean, and Sacred Heart Cemetery. None of these truly warrant their own chapter, but each is an intricate part of the lore of Archer Avenue.

Bethania

In her often repeated attempts to return to Resurrection Cemetery, the ghost of Mary must pass Bethania Cemetery, which borders Resurrection to the south. Although less well-known than its notorious neighbor, Bethania has developed its own reputation for the unusual. In October 1989, the *Southtown Economist* (now known as the *Southtown Star*) reported the arrest of two young men inside Bethania Cemetery in the early morning hours. A day earlier, police had discovered an altar made from a marble cross—probably stolen from a monument—in a wooded area of the cemetery. The cross had been placed inside a circle drawn in the ground, and the police found evidence of a fire at the location. Cemetery workers caught the two young men as they traipsed across the grounds the next day. Police searched the men and found various metaphysical books and items on their persons. The two were charged with trespassing.[1]

Why Not?

On the opposite side of Route 171, along Frontage Road, sits the Why Not drive-in, a greasy spoon that serves typical American fair to its satisfied customers. According to Dale Kaczmarek, president of the Ghost Research Society, a local legend maintains that a ghost named Debbie appears on foggy nights to lure unsuspecting men on a futile chase through the streets of suburban Justice. She parks her 1965 Ford Fairlane in the lot of the Why Not and waits for a young man to pull up next to her. After a brief exchange, Debbie promises that if the man will follow her home, she will accompany him on a date. Excited, the victim tries to follow the mysterious woman's red taillights as her convertible disappears into the fog. If anyone has ever made it home with Debbie, they haven't returned to tell the tale.[2] The Why Not was recently remodeled and opened under new owners.

Justice Public Library

The Justice Public Library is located a few blocks north of the Why Not drive-in, along Oak Grove Avenue. Built in 1995, the new building replaced Justice's older and much smaller library, which Richard T. Crowe, purveyor of Chicago Supernatural Tours, reported to be afflicted with poltergeist activity. When the library moved to its new location just across the street, the ghost moved as well.

Things at the new building were relatively quiet until 1999, when a man named Adrian Dalwood became director of the library. Dalwood reported that books started to be reshelved and stacked after hours. He claimed that a patron, who had pulled into the parking lot at night to make a phone call, witnessed someone removing books from the shelves in the darkness of the library's interior. One theory held that the meddlesome intruder was the ghost of a former member of the library's board of directors who vowed that there would never be a male director of the library as long as she was around. That was a plausible enough explanation for the disturbance, as the activity stopped when Mr. Dalwood accepted a job in Canada.[3] The reorganizing of books seems like an odd activity for a ghost, but as Peter Venkman sarcastically remarked in the movie *Ghostbusters*, "No human being would stack books like this."

Healing Waters Park

Across Archer Avenue on the other side of the Des Plaines River and the Chicago Sanitary and Ship Canal, nestled in a subdivision at the corner of 85th and Willow Drive, lies Healing Waters Park. The park, which consists of a small pond and a row of boulders ninety-two yards in length, is the last vestige of the area's prehistory. Long before the first Europeans set foot on the land that would one day become the village of Willow Springs, the Algonquian peoples traveled to this area to drink from springs that reportedly possessed healing powers.[4] The boulders that mark the location are arranged in a precise north-south direction, with a circle of smaller stones at the southern end. "A circle of boulders contained the ceremonial eternal flame kept burning by the Mascoutin Society, a religious group," a plaque at the park explains. "The Indians came to this place to be cared for until healed."[5] Although the pond and its miraculous waters remain, it is surrounded by a black fence and a sign warns visitors against attempting to collect or drink the water.

Healing Waters Park, Willow Springs.
Photo by the author.

Fairmount Hills Cemetery

Back across the river, exactly one mile southeast of Healing Waters Park nestled between 95th, 104th, and Archer Ave, is Fairmount Hills Cemetery, also known as Willow Hills Memorial Park. Fairmount vaguely resembles the state of Idaho in shape and breaks up the topography of the Archer Avenue "triangle." It is a scenic, garden-like cemetery plotted on rolling hills, but it has not escaped from the area's enigmatic pull. According to Dale Kaczmarek, visitors discovered the body of a young woman inside Fairmount Hills in February 1981. She had been beaten and strangled, but there was no evidence of a robbery. Stranger still, someone broke into the funeral home where her body was awaiting burial and placed a rose and a love note nearby. The case went cold for a year until the woman's ex-boyfriend turned himself in for the crime.[6]

The most frequently retold story associated with the cemetery is that of the mysterious music of the White mausoleum. The mausoleum, which no longer exists, was a simple, rectangular structure perched at the top of a hill with a small staircase that led up to its rusted door. Over the past few decades, several visitors reported hearing eerie music there. On one visit in 1982, a woman named Valerie told Richard Crowe that, "All of a sudden, faint but quite clear, a harpsichord began playing." Both Valerie and her niece heard the ethereal music, but it stopped abruptly when her sister joined them at the steps of the mausoleum.[7] Dale Kaczmarek reported that the music was most often heard at dusk, and that the interior of the mausoleum was filled with concrete a long time ago, eliminating the possibility that the mysterious notes could be coming from a musical device interred with the Whites.[8] Unfortunately, the White mausoleum was heavily damaged in a fire in 2003 and has since been torn down.[9]

95th and Kean Avenue

East of Fairmount Hills Cemetery along 95th Street lies yet another location in the Archer Avenue "triangle," an inconspicuous intersection allegedly haunted by some unusual apparitions. According to a variety of eyewitnesses, ghostly animals have been seen at the intersection of 95th and Kean Avenue near Hidden Pond Woods. The Palos Trail winds its way through these woods between Route 20 and Kean Avenue, and popular opinion holds that a number of horses and their riders have been killed trying to cross 95th Street. Today, the area is not as secluded as it was in the 1970s when motorists began to see the phantoms. Subdivisions are now tightly bunched along the east side of Kean, marking the boundary of the park district, but on one particular night in 1979, a couple named Dennis and Sandy told Richard Crowe, the intersection was dark, remote, and shrouded in fog. It would have been easy enough to fail to notice a living equestrian, but in a few dramatic moments the two narrowly avoided striking a ghostly procession of horses and riders that were illuminated by an eerie glow. Sandy described the figures as "glistening," and told Crowe that she didn't remember seeing their hooves touch the ground.[10]

Horses aren't the only animals to make this intersection their otherworldly home. Just inside the woods at the entrance to the Palos Trail at 95th and Kean sits a small, marble headstone inscribed with the name "Felix." Felix was the beloved mascot of the local fire station who helped save many lives during his tenure with the department. According to Dale Kaczmarek, the ghost of Felix has been seen near the intersection on several occasions.[11]

Felix is not the only canine to have been interred in the area. A little over a mile and a half north, somewhere under the highway that used to be the intersection of Kean and Archer Avenue, is buried the body of Nellie, a black and tan mongrel who served as the mascot of the Willow Springs division of the highway patrol. She was struck and killed by a vehicle in October 1927, leaving behind a litter of pups. Her body was buried "in a wooded field at Archer Avenue and Keane [sic],"[12] an area just north of Archer Woods Cemetery that is now a tangle of exit ramps for the toll road and Route 45.

Sacred Heart Cemetery

Last but not least, there is the strange tale of the "gray-haired baby" of Sacred Heart Cemetery. Sacred Heart is a small graveyard dating back to the time when this area was still dotted by farms. It is located along Kean Avenue in Crooked Creek Woods south of the haunted intersection. 103rd Street dead-ends in front of the cemetery. Out of all the stories in the Archer Avenue "triangle," Sacred Heart might be home to the most incredible. It is the story of the "gray-haired baby," and a feral man (some say a werewolf) who stalks the woods and horse trails nearby. According to Richard Crowe, the legend began in the 1950s when, allegedly, a man and his wife were killed in a car accident near Sacred Heart Cemetery. Their baby was thrown from the vehicle and somehow survived in the forest preserve, feeding off the local wildlife. On moonlit nights, passing motorists occasionally caught a glimpse of a hairy creature in their headlights, and equestrians riding on the nearby trail reported that their horses would be spooked by something unseen.[13]

FELIX
No.2 S.C.F.D.
COMPLEMENTS OF
E.WUNDERLICH GRANITE CO.
79, ARCHER AVE.

The grave of Felix the firedog at 95th and Kean Ave.

Another version of the legend takes a more supernatural turn. A woman named Terrie told Richard Crowe that in the 1970s locals believed that a werewolf was buried in Sacred Heart Cemetery. The belief stemmed from a small, nondescript stone in the corner of the graveyard that appeared to be set apart from the others. Moreover, the fence near this grave had been dramatically bent downward. "Rumor was this was so the werewolf could get in and out," she said.[14] Was it a zombie werewolf desperate to return to his grave? This version of the tale almost makes the story of the feral child seem plausible. After all, there have been documented cases of children raised by animals,[15] but how long could such a person stay hidden at the outskirts of a metropolis like Chicago? Probably not for over five decades. Never the less, there are many who would swear that they encountered something strange and mysterious lurking in the woods around Sacred Heart.

There are many theories as to why this area attracts such a variety of unusual phenomena. In Ursula Bielski's book, *Chicago Haunts*, she explored the possibility that this section of Archer Avenue runs alongside a ley line, metaphysical lines in the earth that intersect at "nodal points." These points were said to attract and concentrate paranormal energy. As Bielski explained, the concept of ley lines originated in England in the early 1900s with a man named Alfred Watkins. Watkins was not a geologist and his theories were never accepted by the scientific community. Never the less, that did not stop people enamored with the concept from roaming the English countryside, mapping the lines. One of these men, a dowser named Guy Underwood, speculated that springs lay under many of the "nodal points."[16] Is it a coincidence that in southwestern Cook County the underground springs that inspired the name "Willow Springs" also feed many of the lakes and sloughs in the Archer Avenue "triangle?" Could they be connected to these mysterious lines? The evidence in favor of that theory is tenuous at best.

Since this portion of Route 171 was built over an old Indian trial, some individuals interested in the paranormal have speculated that Native Americans instinctually knew a ley line existed there. For example, in Scott Markus' book, *Voices from the Chicago Grave*, he wrote, "Archer Avenue was most likely a ley line used by Native Americans so it may be considered sacred ground."[17] Setting aside the tendency of white Americans to ascribe extraordinary spirituality and authenticity to non-European peoples, the land on which Archer Avenue sits is an ideal place for a road. It is at the base of a ridge that follows the Des Plaines River, which would have been a major conduit for trade—a reason why the Illinois Central Rail and the Chicago Sanitary and Ship Canal were also built there. The tip of the ridge, above the modern-day intersection of Route 171 and 107th Street, made an excellent observation point. The first French explorers recognized these attributes when they arrived in the 1700s. It is no wonder that first the Native Americans and then European Americans chose this location for a thoroughfare.

It is more likely that these stories cropped up along this stretch of Archer Avenue because, like Cuba Road north of Chicago, the area developed a reputation for the mysterious among urban residents who came to the lakes, trails, and forest preserves to "get away" from the big city. It is a place where visitors encounter cemeteries tucked inside the woods, lakes that seem to glow in the moonlight, and an old limestone church that looms above the surrounding landscape. In the darkness of night, one could easily imagine hearing the frantic hooves of a phantom black carriage barreling toward Archer Woods Cemetery. There are haunted locations scattered throughout the City of Chicago, but no one place that is sufficiently remote enough to become a breeding ground for those tales. The Archer Avenue "triangle," at the periphery of the collective consciousness of Chicagoland's 9.5 million residents, is such a place. In the following chapters, we will explore the history and folklore of five of the area's most legendary locations.

Chapter Endnotes

[1]*Southtown Economist* (Chicago) 17 October 1989.

[2]Dale Kaczmarek, *Windy City Ghosts: An Essential Guide to the Haunted History of Chicago* (Oak Lawn: Ghost Research Society Press, 2005), 170.

[3]Richard T. Crowe, *Chicago's Street Guide to the Supernatural* (Oak Park: Carolando Press, 2000, 2001), 215.

[4]Jim Graczyk and Donna Boonstra, *Field Guide to Illinois Hauntings* (Alton: Whitechapel Productions Press, 2001), 72-73.

[5]Willow Springs Historical Society, *Untitled Plaque*, 1984, Healing Waters Park, Willow Springs.

[6]Kaczmarek, 85.

[7]Crowe, 234.

[8]Kaczmarek, 86.

[9]Scott Markus, *Voices from the Chicago Grave: They're Calling. Will You Answer?* (Holt: Thunder Bay Press, 2008), 266.

[10]Crowe, 228.

[11]Kaczmarek, 75.

[12]*Daily Tribune* (Chicago) 15 October 1927; *Daily Tribune* (Chicago) 16 October 1927. The original *Tribune* article inaccurately reported that Nellie was laid to rest inside Archer Woods Cemetery.

[13]Crowe, 225.

[14]Ibid., 227.

[15]See: Michael Newton, *Savage Girls and Wild Boys: A History of Feral Children* (New York: Picador, 2004).

[16]Ursula Bielski, *Chicago Haunts: Ghostlore of the Windy City* (Chicago: Lake Claremont Press, 1998), 80-81.

[17]Markus, 282.

Resurrection Cemetery
and the
Legend of Resurrection Mary

Resurrection Mary is undoubtedly Chicagoland's most famous ghost. For over seventy years she has hitched rides from unsuspecting commuters along a dark stretch of Archer Avenue between the Willowbrook Ballroom and Resurrection Cemetery. Always virginal, yet slightly dangerous, Mary has inspired the retelling of her spectral carousing in books, novels, movies, song, and in the dingy taverns of Chicago's southwest side. Yet no one knows if Mary is a real ghost—in the classic sense—or only a localized version of a popular urban legend, the Vanishing Hitchhiker. For decades men and women have poured over documents and testimony, searching for the answer.

Mary's story dates back to the 1930s when the ghost of a burgeoning Polish girl was first seen along Archer Avenue near Resurrection Cemetery. According to Kenan Heise, who would later go on to write a novel about the ghost, "she is a minor cult, a shared belief and an initiation rite for teenagers. When you learn to drive… you test the myth's reality."[1] Richard Crowe originally popularized the story in the 1970s, when he began collecting firsthand accounts and theorized that the real-life Mary had perished in a car accident in the early 1930s. "Mary supposedly was killed in a car wreck 40 years ago, and she's been coming back and going dancing ever since," he remarked in an article in the *Chicago Tribune* in 1974.[2] Later, he elaborated that the sightings usually occurred around 1:30am, and that "women rarely encounter Mary… unless they are with men."[3]

Mary's paraphysical appearance has been disputed over the years, leading some to speculate that more than one ghost may be involved in the story. According to Peter Gorner of the *Chicago Tribune*, Mary materializes as "a pretty Polish girl, about 18, with long blonde hair, wearing a white dancing dress."[4] Michael Norman and Beth Scott more or less agreed, calling her specter a "captivating, blue-eyed, flaxen-haired girl in her late teens" who wears a "long, off-white ballgown and dancing shoes."[5]

According to Ursula Bielski, however, Mary "wore a beautiful white party dress and patent leather dancing shoes."[6] In the mind of Jo-Anne Christensen, Mary is a "breathtaking blonde with light blue eyes, dressed elegantly in a snowy white cocktail dress with matching satin dancing shoes."[7] In his *Haunted Illinois*, Troy Taylor added a "thin shawl" to her appearance.[8] Rachel Brooks romantically portrayed Mary as "an innocent young woman... stranded and alone." She is "soaked to the bone... with beautiful blonde hair and sparkling blue eyes."[9] In Kenan Heise's novel, Mary was a young woman dressed in "a gown of a thin, chiffon-like material," or a "long, white gown with a cape."[10]

With so many wardrobe changes, readers are liable to conclude that there must be a supernatural Macy's out there. However, it is not uncommon for eyewitnesses to give varying descriptions of living persons they had just seen moments ago, let alone ghosts, so there is plenty of room for speculation.

Despite some minor disagreements, it is generally acknowledged that Mary sightings first began in the 1930s. In 1936, a man named Jerry Palus picked up a mysterious girl at the Liberty Grove Hall and Ballroom in Brighton Park. She instructed him to drive her down Archer Avenue and asked to be let out near Resurrection Cemetery. The young woman reportedly told him something to the effect of, "where I'm going you cannot follow," before she disappeared through the gates. Years later, Jerry's brother Chester would claim that a friend, and not Jerry, had been driving the car that night.[11]

Other early sightings included the specter of Mary causing a scene as she threw herself at passing cars. Over the years, Mary would resort to materializing as an accident victim, always vanishing as the bewildered drivers got out of their cars to survey the damage. This bloody behavior either shows two ghosts at work, as Richard Crowe suggested in *Chicago's Street Guide to the Supernatural*, or it shows that the ghost of Mary cannot be pigeonholed so easily as just another urban legend.

In July 1979, the *Tribune* published a letter that claimed the last time the ghost of Mary had been seen was in August 1976 or '77, by two policemen near the gate of Resurrection Cemetery.[12] That anonymous writer was probably referring to the most intriguing event of all related to this saga: the night that Mary left physical evidence behind.

Although most accounts of the incident vaguely refer to a "man" or "someone" at "some time" having seen a woman in white clasping the bars of the cemetery gate, Richard Crowe revealed that the man in question was none other than Pat Homa, a Justice police officer who had responded to a trespassing call the night of August 10, 1976 and discovered two of the bars burnt and bent irregularly, with what looked like finger impressions melted into the bronze.[13]

As crowds began to gather, the Cemetery Board tried to smooth the bars with blowtorches, which only made the "handprints" more conspicuous. Finally, the caretakers removed the bars altogether and sent them off to be straightened. According to Crowe, the bars were put back in December 1978, but the discoloration remained. Officially, the

Willowbrook Ballroom,
dancehall of Resurrection Mary.

incident originated in an accident involving cemetery workers who had accidentally backed into the gate with a truck. The "handprints" were made when one of the workers tried to bend it back into place using a blow torch and heavy-duty gloves.[14]

Chet's Melody Lounge

Sightings of Mary, along with ghostly phenomena attributed to her presence, continue to this day, especially amongst the patrons of Chet's Melody Lounge, a large pub located across the street from Resurrection Cemetery. Every weekend, its bartenders leave a Bloody Mary at the end of the bar in case the ghost makes an appearance. "A lot of my friends have felt someone tap them on the shoulder when they were the only person in the bar. They turn around: nothing," Tony Zaleski, a longtime employee at Chet's, told Michael McCarty and Connie Corcoran Wilson. "Or someone behind them will ruffle their collar and they feel a chill."[15] In 1973 a cab driver is said to have burst into Chet's demanding to know where the blonde went that had left him waiting outside. He was rebuffed by the employees, who told him that no such woman had come inside that night.

Still More Marys

Mary's earthly origins are as elusive as her ghost, and several historical candidates have been put forward. A commonly articulated candidate was a twenty-one-year-old woman named Mary Bregovy, who died in a car accident while (allegedly) returning home from the O'Henry Ballroom on March 11, 1934. Mary Bregovy died in downtown Chicago, however, nowhere near Resurrection Cemetery, even though she was interred there. Also, this Mary had short, dark or brown hair and was buried in an orchid dress. According to Ursula Bielski, a cemetery worker had told a nearby funeral director that he had seen Bregovy's ghost in Resurrection Cemetery during the 1950s. Apparently the two stories became enmeshed and Bregovy was henceforth regarded as Mary's physical and historical counterpart.[16]

A second candidate was one Mary Miskowski, who was struck by a car and killed on her way to a Halloween party sometime in the 1930s. Another Mary died in a car accident in the 1940s, Chad Lewis and Terry Fisk recently reported, but as they pointed out, the first sightings of the ghost occurred a decade earlier.[17]

The least likely candidate for Resurrection Mary was a twelve year old Lithuanian girl named Anna Norkus, who took on Marija, "Mary," as a favored middle name. She was killed in a car accident on her way to the O'Henry Ballroom on July 20, 1927. Her existence as a ghost, according to Bielski, largely depends on a "what if" scenario that might have resulted in her body being mistakenly laid to rest in an unmarked grave in Resurrection Cemetery. Mary the ghost, however, is always described as either at least the age of maturity or between seventeen and twenty-one, not a young girl of twelve.

To skeptics and folklorists, the story of Resurrection Mary is obviously a retelling of the popular urban legend, "The Vanishing Hitchhiker." Jan Harold Brunvand, who wrote a book on the subject, explained, "'The Vanishing Hitchhiker' has international distribution as one of the oldest and most widely told of all urban legends, as such, it has long attracted the attention of folklore scholars."[18] Brunvand noted that, in the United States, the story often takes the form of a mysterious young woman who gets a ride home from her dancing partner, only to vanish before arriving. In some versions, the unlucky man finds his sweater draped over her headstone after being informed that she died in a car accident years before. In Alvin Schwartz's retelling of the tale, the item recovered is Christmas tinsel.[19]

Christmas is an important element to the story, because many of the sightings of Resurrection Mary allegedly occurred in wintertime. In *Chicago Ghosts*, Ursula Bielski related the story of a taxi driver who picked up a young woman (Mary) outside of a shopping center in January. He was surprised by the girl's dress, which was inadequate for the cold. "The snow came early this year," she told him before vanishing.[20] As in the version of the "The Vanishing Hitchhiker" where the man's sweater was left on her grave, the mysterious girl wore a dress without a coat in spite of the season. The fact that Mary commented on the weather in January, as though she was surprised that it was snowing, indicated that, at least in her world, it was still not quite the dead of winter.

The comment about the weather, alongside Mary's other eerie final remarks, also reflect a similarity with "The Vanishing Hitchhiker." In other parts of the country, such as along I-29 in South Dakota and Route 61 in Pennsylvania, the phantom hitchhiker told his startled benefactors that the world was going to end.[21] In those tales, the hitchhiker remained stoic through most of the drive, just like Mary. "Quiet and non-talkative," as Richard Crowe described her.[22]

That some authors claim Jerry Palus, the first man to have reported an encounter with Mary, went the following morning to the address she had given him to see if she had made it home okay, only to have an old woman inform him that her daughter had died years before, should be familiar to students of "The Vanishing Hitchhiker."[23] That particular detail is alternatively ascribed to or omitted from different Mary encounters, suggesting that the line between the urban legend and eyewitness accounts often disappears.

But some of Mary's behavior, such as throwing herself in front of oncoming cars or putting on similar bloody displays, do not match the urban legend, so which came first, the ghost stories or the legend? Did the legend inspire the ghost stories, or did the ghost stories inspire the legend? In truth, they probably possess a symbiotic relationship. Every time a young woman named Mary met her fate along Archer Avenue in the early twentieth century, someone tied her death to the stories of a vanishing hitchhiker along the road. Real events or cases of mistaken identity reinforced the stories, until they became uniquely Chicagoan, especially in ascribing a Polish ancestry to the ghost. In the end, the connection between our ghost and the urban legend blurred, if not vanished, in our minds.

It is worth noting that Mary is not the only phantom hitchhiker in Chicago. Many annals of local ghostlore also relate the story of the "flapper" ghost of North Riverside's Melody Mill Ballroom and Jewish Waldheim Cemetery. Like Mary, this young woman died in the 1920s or the early '30s and her ghost danced the night away with strangers, vanishing on her ride home, but unlike Mary, she dressed much more flamboyantly and possessed brunette, "bobbed" hair.[24] The ballroom was eventually demolished, but sightings of the flapper continued into the '90s.

Whoever or whatever Resurrection Mary was in the past or is today, her legacy will always remain as one of the most beloved specters of Chicagoland. She is our own romantic fantasy—a forlorn young woman, draped in a thin gown, wandering the dark avenues looking for help from her knight in shining armor. As long as the wind whips down Archer Avenue, writers, musicians, folklorists, ghost hunters, and surprised motorists will continue to reinvent and retell her story for generations to come.

Chapter Endnotes

[1]*Chicago Tribune* (Chicago) 29 October 1982.

[2]*Chicago Tribune* (Chicago) 13 May 1974.

[3]*Chicago Tribune* (Chicago) 31 October 1985.

[4]*Chicago Tribune* (Chicago) 13 May 1974.

[5]Beth Scott and Michael Norman, *Haunted Heartland: True Ghost Stories from the American Midwest* (New York: Barnes & Noble Books, 1985, 1992), 1.

[6]Ursula Bielski, *Chicago Haunts: Ghostlore of the Windy City* (Chicago: Lake Claremont Press, 1998), 23.

[7]Jo-Anne Christensen, *Ghost Stories of Illinois* (Edmonton: Lone Pine, 2000), 48.

[8]Troy Taylor, *Haunted Illinois: Travel Guide to the History and Hauntings of the Prairie State* (Alton: Whitechapel Productions Press, 2004), 336.

[9]Rachel Brooks, *Chicago Ghosts* (Atglen: Schiffer Books, 2008), 41.

[10]Kenan Heise, *Resurrection Mary: a Ghost Story* (Evanston: Chicago Historical Bookworks, 1990), 20.

[11]Bielski, 17.

[12]*Chicago Tribune* (Chicago) 2 July 1979.

[13]Richard T. Crowe, *Chicago's Street Guide to the Supernatural* (Oak Park: Carolando Press, 2000, 2001), 219.

[14]Bielski, 22.

[15]Michael McCarty and Connie Corcoran Wilson, *Ghostly Tales of Route 66: from Chicago to Oklahoma* (Wever: Quixote Press, 2008), 18.

[16]Bielski, 15.

[17]Chad Lewis and Terry Fisk, *The Illinois Road Guide to Haunted Locations* (Eau Claire: Unexplained Research Publishing, 2007), 113.

[18]Jan Harold Brunvand, *Too Good to be True: the Colossal Book of Urban Legends* (New York: W.W. Norton & Company, 1999, 2001), 234.

[19]*Scary Stories Treasury: Three Books to Chill Your Bones*, Alvin Schwartz, *More Scary Stories to Tell in the Dark* (New York: Harper Collins, 1984), 5.

[20]Bielski, 23.

[21]Brunvand, 232.

[22]Crowe, 223.

[23]Taylor, 339; Lewis and Fisk, 111; Brooks, 49.

[24]Crowe, 190.

Archer Woods Cemetery and the Specter of the Sobbing Woman

Archer Woods Cemetery is located at 8301 Kean Avenue next to Lithuanian Cemetery, across the street from Buffalo Woods. Separated from Archer Avenue by the Tri State Tollway and the US Route 45 exit and entrance ramps, it is nestled at the end of Kean Avenue between the forest preserve and a series of isolated businesses and horse stables. There the traffic disappears and the graveyard takes on the feeling of having been forgotten by the outside world. This tranquility is deceptive, however, and authors like Ursula Bielski warn their readers that local residents "consider this cemetery the most foreboding of Archer Avenue's four burial grounds."[1] The folklore of Archer Woods concerns both a sobbing woman in white and the specter of a black hearse, which may be two of the earliest stories in the area.

There is no recorded explanation for either of those tales, at least not that this author has found, but the history of the cemetery might offer clues as to why it has attracted such a negative reputation. Established in 1920, just nine years after the neighboring village of Justice, Archer Woods contains the remains of many of the area's German residents. In addition to the mourned and cared for, the unknown and the unwanted were also interred there beneath the white oaks.

A Mortician's Scandal

In the summer of 1950, a scandal broke at Archer Woods that involved two morticians, John Regan and Adolph Cohn, who accepted money from the county to bury six old-age pensioners—men who died without families or savings—in the cemetery.[2] State and county law required that all bodies be properly embalmed, dressed, and buried in coffins. Acting on a court order obtained by Judge John Lupe, the Assistant State's Attorney exhumed the bodies of the men. A doctor representing the County Coroner in the case determined that five of the six had been buried without clothing and without being embalmed. All of the men had been placed in small, pine boxes. The Assistant State's Attorney "indicated he may seek warrants… against the two undertakers who buried the bodies and received fees from the state and county," the *Daily Tribune* reported.[3] In April 1951, Regan and Cohn appeared in court and were charged with conspiracy to defraud the state of $100 to $120 for each burial.[4] It was a ghoulish crime worthy of the pages of *Tales from the Crypt*. In its coverage of the trial, the local newspaper did not reveal whether the bodies of the men in question had ever been given a proper burial. It seemed as though the six pensioners had been forgotten in the drama of the moment

Potter's Field

During the 1970s, Archer Woods Cemetery served as the county's potter's field, where the bodies of the anonymous dead, or those too poor to afford a plot or a funeral, were interred. "We hold 'em until we get enough to make a run, about 30 or 32, and then we bury them in what I'd call a ditch type thing," the administrator for the Cook County medical examiner told *Chicago Tribune* reporter Sam Smith. Each coffin was given a number before being lowered into an unmarked grave. "Such is the fate of society's forgotten, the lonely and deserted, the alcoholics, the drifters, the destitute," Smith wrote. "They find their final resting places in suburban fields, in long ditches marked by posts and the absence of flowers or headstones."[5] Such was the fate of an unidentified man who intervened in a fight outside of the Wilson Club hotel in 1974. His actions saved the lives of three teenagers, but not his own. An enraged man, who had been threatening the teens with a knife, ran him down and stabbed him to death. His body lay unidentified for ninety days, and was thus given a nondescript burial somewhere on the grounds of Archer Woods Cemetery.[6] Perhaps it is the spirits of these unknown souls that give the graveyard its forlorn atmosphere?

Woman in White

In addition to the grieving relatives of the deceased, there are those who come to Archer Woods in search of its otherworldly residents and many report feelings of unease. On one visit, Scott Marcus, the owner of Slim Pictures and former co-host of the "Mothership Connection" on WLIP AM-1050, related, "Upon entering the front gate, one becomes immediately cautious of the rough grounds and deteriorating roads. Many of the trees are dead... There is a basic feeling that all is not right here." His feelings were confirmed when his companions and he discovered a large tree that had been adorned with various objects. A stuffed animal and a maple syrup bottle hung from the branches, and a teddy bear had been nailed to the trunk approximately five yards

The gates of
Woods Cemetery.

CEMETERY NOT
RESPONSIBLE
FOR ACCIDENTS
OR INJURIES TO
VISITORS OR
THEIR PROPERTY

CEMETERY
BY HOURS OR
DAILY 8:00 A.M.–4:00 P.M.
OFFICE HOURS
BY APPOINTMENT ONLY
PLEASE CALL (708) 839-8800
THANK YOU

from the ground. "As far as we were concerned, this was evidence of cultists practicing their craft or at the very least some people with bad intentions who visit the cemetery," Markus wrote.[7]

Cultists with a furry fetish and a hatred for pancakes aside, the story most frequently associated with the cemetery is that of a weeping woman in white. There are many similar stories at other cemeteries in the Chicagoland area, most notably at Bachelor's Grove in Midlothian. Just like at Bachelor's Grove, the weeping woman of Archer Woods wanders through the trees, wailing and pulling her hair, but unlike the ghost who searches Bachelor's Grove for her missing child, the motivation of Archer Woods' phantom is less clear. According to Trent Brandon's *Book of Ghosts*, the weeping woman is a type of ghost he calls "The Broken Heart." Having lost one dear to them, "they are waiting alone and desperately searching for the soul of a dead child or waiting the return of their true love," he explained. "They can be heard weeping sadly and singing gloomy songs." The ghost, most often a woman, is overwhelmed with guilt for her dead child or lover and believes she must wander the earth endlessly until reunited, or until she has endured enough punishment to assuage her guilt.[8]

Could the weeping woman of Archer Woods be searching for the grave of a child or a man who was buried in one the many anonymous plots? Chroniclers of the area's folklore are mute on that point. Ursula Bielski, who wrote extensively on Archer Avenue, failed to provide any motivation for or accounts of the haunting. Scott Markus, on the other hand, related in his work a secondhand encounter with the weeping woman given to him by two Hickory Hills police officers. The two claimed to have known a fellow patrolman who went out to Archer Woods Cemetery one evening to investigate a disturbance. "As the officer was looking around the cemetery grounds, a semi-transparent woman dressed in white ran past him screaming," Markus wrote. "That officer then retired or transferred."[9]

The weeping/sobbing woman, otherwise known as a "woman in white," is a common folklore motif. In Germany, they tell the tale of the *Weisse Frauen* ("white women"), a holdover from pre-Christian times. Although many of the area residents are of German extraction, *Weisse Frauen* are associated with elves and other mythical beings. The ghost of the woman who haunts Archer Woods more closely approximates the Spanish legend of *La Llorona* ("the weeping woman"). In the United States, *La Llorona* is most frequently encountered in the southwest. According to New Mexico lore, a poor woman named Maria fell in love with a wealthy ranchero who believed her to be the most beautiful woman he had ever seen. The two wed and Maria bore him three children. As time went on, the man grew tired of his wife and his eyes began to wander. In a jealous rage, Maria took her children to the Rio Grande and drowned them. Learning of her crime, her husband cast her out of his house. Maria spent the rest of her life—as well as her afterlife—roaming the river, wailing and searching for her children. She had become *La Llorona*. It was said that *La Llorona* would abduct any children who were unlucky enough to be caught near the river after dark.[10] Until very recently, however, the residents of Chicago's southwest suburbs have been of Polish, Irish, and German decent, not Hispanic. It is unlikely that the legend of *La Llorona* was the inspiration for the weeping woman of Archer Woods, despite the similarity. The true origin of this phantom was likely lost long ago in the murky depths of the folk history of Archer Avenue.

The Black Hearse

Even more fantastic than the woman in white is the tale of the phantom black hearse that is alleged to rocket past the cemetery. No description other than that given by Kenan Heise in his novel, *Resurrection Mary: A Ghost Story*, could do it justice: "The sepulchral apparition's shiny wooden frame is of the blackest oak. Its glass sides shimmer in what little moonlight there is, exposing in outline the white coffin of a child. There is no driver... The terror of the hearse rips a hole in the soul of everyone who has encountered it."[11] In addition, two gas lamps are said to hang from the terrifying carriage.

The hearse appears at various points along Archer Avenue, transporting its frail cargo to parts unknown. According to Ursula Bielski, some eyewitnesses have linked the phantom hearse to the legend of Resurrection Mary. Mary's parents, the storytellers claimed, swore off modern modes of transportation and chose an old-fashioned, horse-drawn carriage for their daughter's body.[12] But if Mary's body was taken to her final resting place in a hearse, why does she still hitchhike to Resurrection Cemetery all these years later? Also, the coffin in the phantom hearse is said to contain the body of a young child. Perhaps it is the body of the son or daughter of the sobbing woman of Archer Woods? The origin of this legend is as elusive as the last, but there is an older story, predating the existence of Archer Woods Cemetery, that will be discussed in our chapter on St. James-Sag that may hold the answer.

Garden of Hymns

There is one more story associated with Archer Woods, much younger than the sobbing woman or the phantom hearse. The story concerns an unusual monument on the west side of the cemetery entitled "Garden of Hymns." The monument consists of several metal pipes jutting from a base made of stones and vaguely resembles a pipe organ. Recently, some visitors have reported hearing the faint sound of organ music emanating from the area. "It was eerie, like a low hum," Jen, who asked to remain anonymous because she was in the cemetery after dark, wrote in an e-mail to me in 2007. "We couldn't figure out where it was coming from until we saw that organ."[13] Archer Woods Cemetery is not as remote as it seems, however, and there are many places where such a sound could originate. That hasn't stopped the rumors from spreading, and the Internet has made it much easier for these stories to take on a life of their own.

There must be a reason why, despite their proximity and their nearly identical landscape, Archer Woods has attracted these legends and not its neighbor, Lithuanian Cemetery. The existence of the potter's field might be one explanation. Perhaps it is the local memory of the many unseemly things that have transpired in the cemetery in the past, or simply because the cemetery shares a name with the infamous road. Whatever the reason, Archer Woods has cemented its association with the lore of Archer Avenue—for better or for worse.

Chapter Endnotes

[1]Ursula Bielski, *Chicago Haunts: Ghostlore of the Windy City* (Chicago: Lake Claremont Press, 1998), 73.
[2]*Daily Tribune* (Chicago) 14 June 1950.
[3]*Daily Tribune* (Chicago) 17 June 1950.
[4]*Daily Tribune* (Chicago) 17 April 1951.
[5]*Chicago Tribune* (Chicago) 1 February 1981.
[6]*Chicago Tribune* (Chicago) 4 November 1974; *Chicago Tribune* (Chicago) 21 November 1974.
[7]Scott Markus, *Voices from the Chicago Grave: They're Calling. Will You Answer?* (Holt: Thunder Bay Press, 2008), 283-284.
[8]Trent Brandon, *The Book of Ghosts* (Galloway: Zerotime Publishing, 2003), 87.
[9]Markus, 285.
[10]*El Defensor Chieftain* (Socorro) 1 December 2007; Rachel Brooks, *Chicago Ghosts* (Atglen: Schiffer Books, 2008), 138-142.
[11]Kenan Heise, *Resurrection Mary: A Ghost Story* (Evanston: Chicago Historical Bookworks, 1990), 25.
[12]Bielski, 24.
[13]Anonymous, "Archer cem music?," personal email (15 November 2007).

German Church Road and the Grimes Sisters' Tragedy

German Church is a nondescript avenue running between Willow Springs Road and County Line Road, just a half-mile north of Healing Waters Park. The area is sparsely populated and two streams, Flag and Devil's Creek, gently wind their way through the nearby woods. During the 1950s, not very many people had a reason to venture out to that particular edge of Cook County, but it was along an isolated stretch of German Church Road near Devil's Creek on a cold day in January 1957 when a passing motorist discovered the remains of Barbara and Patricia Grimes. The two sisters had been missing for three weeks before a Hinsdale man named Leonard Prescott noticed their nude bodies lying on the outside of the guard rail just before the culvert leading down to Devil's Creek. Upon identifying the girl's remains, their father, a truck driver named Joseph, exclaimed, "I tried to tell the police my daughters didn't run away, but they wouldn't listen to me."[1]

An End of Innocence

It was the end of a long and exhaustive search, but only the beginning of a case that would shock and fascinate Chicago for decades to come. Many writers have declared that moment to be the end of innocence, but it was, in fact, only one in a series of similar incidents stretching back a decade. The deaths of the Grimes sisters were preceded by the murder of three Chicago-area boys whose nude bodies were found in Robinson Woods in 1955. Three other boys disappeared near Minneapolis, Minnesota, in 1950. They were dramatic instances in a long and painful string of child murders around the Midwest. At the time of the discovery of the Grimes sisters, none of these crimes had been solved.

In the decades since the girl's remains were found, many strange stories have been told regarding that lonely stretch of German Church Road. Some involved the ruins of a nearby house the owner abandoned soon after the murders, and which has since been torn down. The other stories concern eerie sounds and phantom automobiles that seem to reenact the day Barbara and Patricia were dumped along the side of the road. None of those experiences can be properly understood, however, without first delving into the circumstances surrounding the unusual case of the Grimes sisters.

It was the end of 1956. Dwight D. Eisenhower had recently defeated Adlai Stevenson in the US presidential race, and the Suez Crisis ended as British and French troops withdrew from the Suez Canal. Barbara and Patricia Grimes, ages fifteen and thirteen, left their Chicago home on December 28, 1956, to watch *Love Me Tender* at the Brighton Theater on Archer Avenue. Patricia was a fanatical fan of Elvis Presley, who starred in the movie. No one knows if the girls even made it to the theater, although a friend of Barbara's told police she had last seen the pair at the intersection of Archer Avenue and Hamilton Street.[2] Their mother, Loretta Grimes, reported them missing after they failed to return home. Loretta and her husband, Joseph, had divorced eleven years earlier and had four other children besides Barbara and Patricia. By all accounts, the girls were happy and gave no indication that they planned to run away.

Mysterous Findings

When their bodies were finally discovered along the roadside it was after a warm period that melted the snow, leading police to believe that the bodies had laid there for several days, perhaps even more than a week. The initial autopsy only deepened the mystery. The examining pathologist did not find any outward signs of violence that would explain a cause of death, nor did he find any signs of rape. Dr. Jerry Kearns, one of the examining physicians, told the *Daily Tribune*, "it was the first time in his memory that the cause or evidence of death was concealed so well on victims known to have met a violent end." Patricia, however, was found to have several puncture wounds on her chest three-fourths of an inch deep. While not mortal blows, the wounds would have been painful and might have been signs of torture. Additionally, "the condition of the bodies led [police] to believe the bodies were not kept in a warm place for any length of time between the hour of death and the time they were dumped alongside German Church Road," the *Tribune* reported.

In a bizarre twist, the first suspect in the case, a man named Walter Kranz, made an anonymous call to the police two weeks after the disappearance saying that he knew where the girl's remains would be found. After Leonard Prescott stumbled upon the actual dumping site, police tracked down Kranz and administered a lie detector test. Kranz passed. He denied having killed the girls and said their final resting place had appeared to him in a dream. His prediction hadn't been too far off—he told police the bodies of the girls were located in a park a mile and a half south of where they were eventually found.[3]

With practically the whole of Chicago on the lookout for the Grimes sisters between December 29 and January 22, police were inundated with possible sightings that came in from far flung areas of the city. There were tens of thousands of young girls who matched the description of Barbara and Patricia. In fact, twelve other girls were reported missing in Chicago during the month of January, all between the ages of twelve and sixteen.[4] Every lead had to be followed and every possible suspect interrogated, but none seemed to bring investigators any closer to solving the crime. Then, on January 27, the district attorney formerly charged Edward Bedwell, an illiterate twenty-one-year old ne'er-do-well, with the murder of Barbara and Patricia Grimes. Bedwell signed a fourteen-page confession and reenacted the crime for the police, but portions of his confession were contradicted by the autopsy, which showed that one of the girls had an empty stomach while Bedwell claimed both had consumed alcohol and hotdogs shortly before they died.

Bedwell's confession chronicled how he and a man named Frank picked up the girls and took them to various taverns and hotels before ultimately knocking them unconscious and leaving them on the side of the road. "Frank" turned out to be William Cole Willingham, who swore that he never saw the Grimes sisters. Furthermore, he proved beyond a shadow of a doubt that he had been working at the time Bedwell claimed they stayed at hotels with the two girls, and that he was an alcoholic who hadn't driven a car for over a year.[5] Just days later, Bedwell's confession unraveled and he formally recanted. "I was getting scared of getting roughed up then," he told the press. "I didn't know what to do... so I decided I better tell them what they wanted to know." He accused the Chief of the Sheriff's Police of beating him into making the confession. The Sheriff denied abusing the subject and stood by his personal conviction that Bedwell was the murderer.[6]

Early in February, the Cook County Coroner announced that the Grimes sisters had died of exposure to cold. Even after weeks of testing, pathologists could not find one single piece of evidence that would indicate a violent end, nor did the girls appear to have been rendered unconscious before they wound up naked on the side of the road. Furthermore, the pathologists determined that two of the three wounds found on Patricia occurred post-mortem when her body was bitten by rodents. At one point, the Cook County Sheriff was heard arguing with the examining physicians. He insisted there had to have been some kind of foul play. "Those girls were found nude in the woods," the *Tribune* reporter overheard. "They didn't just walk there."[7]

Or did they?

A jury soon ruled that Barbara and Patricia were murdered despite the findings of medical experts. "We the jury are unable to determine how, when, where, or under what circumstances said body or bodies were subjected to conditions causing death," they declared. "However, from the testimony presented, we the jury find said act to be murder."[8] The charges against Edward Bedwell were eventually dropped due to lack of evidence, and the case, like the bodies of Barbara and Patricia Grimes, went cold.

A Legend is Born

Soon after Patricia and Barbara were found, the family living in the house adjacent to the crime scene disappeared leaving everything behind, even their car. Whether they fled to avoid scrutiny in the case, the media circus, or because they couldn't bear to live there after what had happened, no one ever found out. The property owners denied every interview request even as vandals and those with more sinister intentions slowly took over their home. In the 1970s, Richard Crowe went to what became known as the "Grimes girls' house" to investigate the rumors he had heard as a teacher at Lourdes High School. "Visiting the spot with some of my students, I did find the ruins of a large home and evidence to back up this fascinating story," he wrote. "There were pieces of furniture, children's toys and appliances strewn about, and food in the kitchen. There was even a 1956 Buick convertible in the garage…"[9]

After a while, the house was nothing more than a shell covered by graffiti—some of it Satanic. Vandals finally burnt down the wooden part of the structure sometime in the 1990s, leaving a blackened foundation. Despite the destruction of the house, visitors continued to report strange encounters. In *Haunted Illinois*, Troy Taylor related that "while the owner never lived there again, people would occasionally see a tall, gaunt man roaming about the property in the spring and fall."[10] By the time I made it out to the property in 2003, there was nothing left but a pile of rubble and a weed-choked driveway. My friend and I thought it strange that a stone grotto was tucked away in the woods near Devil's Creek, but otherwise the area seemed innocuous. All traces of the gruesome discovery forty-six years earlier had vanished.

Not so, according to a number of eyewitnesses who have reported seeing or hearing phantom automobiles along German Church Road near the place where the Grimes sisters were found. In *Windy City Ghosts*, Dale Kaczmarek explained, "For those people living nearby it's been a common occurrence to hear the sounds of a car screeching to a halt in front of the guardrails in the dead of the night. They hear the car open its doors, something landing in the weeds, the doors shut and then the car peeling away."[11] Ursula Bielski entertained the notion that these were auditory hallucinations brought on by previous knowledge of the case, but Richard Crowe retold a story in which the participants, on a trip to the abandoned house in 1982, witnessed a car come up the driveway without its headlights. The group scattered, only to discover that a metal cable was still strung across the entrance to the driveway, preventing any vehicles from entering.[12]

From where do these ghostly manifestations originate? In his book, *Voices from the Chicago Grave*, Scott Markus theorized that the killer's guilt—whoever or wherever he might be—causes him to dwell on the murders to this very day. "As this event haunts him, it manifests itself in a visual or auditory form," he explained.[13] Like Mr. Markus, the witnesses to this ghostly phenomenon assume the Grimes sisters were murdered and then dumped onto the side of the road, but there is no evidence to support that notion. As pathologists reported at the time, the girls had no mortal wounds, nor had they ingested anything life threatening. They could have walked for at least a half an hour before they succumbed to the cold.

But what were the girls doing without clothes a few yards away from the border between Cook and DuPage County? How did they get there? This mystery, like that of the abandoned property near Devil's Creek and the phantom automobiles along German Church Road, may never be solved. Until the one responsible for their disappearance steps forward, the deaths of Barbara and Patricia Grimes will remain a gruesome stain on the history of a region already haunted by the past.

Chapter Endnotes

[1]*Daily Tribune* (Chicago) 23 January 1957.
[2]*Daily Tribune* (Chicago) 1 January 1957.
[3]*Daily Tribune* (Chicago) 24 January 1957.
[4]*Daily Tribune* (Chicago) 25 January 1957.
[5]*Daily Tribune* (Chicago) 29 January 1957.
[6]*Daily Tribune* (Chicago) 31 January 1957.
[7]*Daily Tribune* (Chicago) 9 February 1957.
[8]*Daily Tribune* (Chicago) 12 January 1957.
[9]Richard T. Crowe, *Chicago's Street Guide to the Supernatural* (Oak Park: Carolando Press, 2000, 2001), 244.
[10]Troy Taylor, *Haunted Illinois: The Travel Guide to the History & Hauntings of the Prairie State* (Alton: Whitechapel Productions Press, 2004), 263.
[11]Dale Kaczmarek, *Windy City Ghosts: An Essential Guide to the Haunted History of Chicago* (Oak Lawn: Ghost Research Society Press, 2005), 89-90.
[12]Ursula Bielski, *Chicago Haunts: Ghostlore of the Windy City* (Chicago: Lake Claremont Press, 1998), 144; Crowe, 244.
[13]Scott Markus, *Voices from the Chicago Grave: They're Calling. Will You Answer?* (Holt: Thunder Bay Press, 2008), 244.

The Maple Lake Spook Lights

Every spring and summer, visitors by the hundreds of thousands descend on the southwestern corner of Cook County. They come to the Palos and Sag Valley Divisions of the Park District to ride horses, hike, and bicycle on the trails, or to drop a fishing line into one of the dozen lakes and sloughs. Many grab a quick bite at the Ashbury Coffee House before heading south down Archer Avenue to 95th Street. There they enter Pulaski Woods under a canopy of maple trees and continue east until they reach Maple Lake, a man-made body of water roughly half a mile in width. With its wide, curving shores and tranquil waters, it is a deceptively peaceful place.

Over the years, Maple Lake has acquired a reputation for the unusual. A handful of visitors—those who stuck around after sundown—have reported seeing strange lights hovering over the lake. These lights, although they are the subject of speculation by every chronicler of Chicagoland folklore, are just the tip of the iceberg. Maple Lake has a grim history into which few have delved. I have been able to confirm at least six deaths in and around the lake, most of which involved drowning, but two were homicides. During the 1960s and '70s, brawls near the lake forced the closure of the forest preserve, and several attacks have occurred in the nearby woods.

Three Men and a Dog

According to at least one author, tragedy scarred the land on which the lake would one day rest. Though the author, Troy Taylor, failed to disclose the source of his information, he claimed that the origin of the Maple Lake ghost light could be found in an accident that took the lives of three men and a dog fifty-six years before the creation of the lake. "The land where Maple Lake now rests was once owned by an Irish immigrant named James Molony," he began. Like many others, Molony came to the United States from Ireland in the early 1850s to escape the potato famine and to make a new life for himself. Taylor claimed that Molony set up shop as a supplier to the thousands of workers who were clearing the way for the Illinois and Michigan Canal, but construction of the canal began in 1836 and was completed in 1848, years before Molony supposedly arrived.[1] Regardless, as the story went, Molony managed to save enough money to purchase an eighty-acre tract of nearby land.

The first place he chose to build his new home was a low area that would one day become the lake bottom. On an October afternoon in 1858, after a morning of celebration at a local christening, Molony and several of his friends went to inspect the well he had dug. One after another, three of the men were lowered into the well and were overcome with gasses that escaped from the swampy soil. Finally, Molony and his remaining companions lowered a stray dog down into the well to see if there was any hope of saving their friends. The dog, unfortunately, also died. "After the horrific loss of his three friends, Molony had the well filled in and he built his house on one of the hills across the basin," Taylor concluded. "He wanted nothing more to do with this cursed piece of ground."[2]

Whatever the land's early history, the Park District purchased it in the early 1920s and built a dam to control the region's water resources. The low area east of the intersection of 95th Street and Wolf Road filled with water and the resulting kidney-shaped lake was named "Maple Lake" after the abundance of sugar maple trees on the surrounding hills. Although there have been deaths there in the eighty-five years since the lake's creation, the claim that "Police and forest rangers have found a number of bodies, mostly young woman" is a bit of an exaggeration.[3] In fact, I was able to find only one recorded instance of a female found dead in or around Maple Lake. The rest were male.

A Dangerous Place

The first recorded instance of a drowning in Maple Lake occurred on June 15, 1930. Stanley Suja, age twenty, and three of his friends were swimming in the lake when, for an undisclosed reason, Stanley met his fate in the tranquil waters.[4] Four years later, again in June, a twenty-seven year old named William Geisler drowned while his wife of four days watched from the shoreline. The two had evidently just finished eating and William was seized by a cramp. His bride managed to get him to shore and someone summoned the paramedics. They tried to revive him for an hour, but to no avail.[5] A month later, Paul Pahnke disappeared while swimming in the lake. Police found his body the next morning.[6]

Contrary to reports in several books on Chicago ghostlore, Maple Lake was not closed to swimming in 1939, but was in fact closed in the summer of 1936. In June of that year the *Daily Tribune* reported, "Pol-

Maple Lake.

luted water, dangerous to the health of swimmers, has caused the closing of Maple Lake at Wolf Road and 95th Street, for bathing purposes." The lake apparently contained high amounts of bacteria due to "lack of adequate feeder springs" that caused typhoid fever, dysentery, and various infections.[7] The ban did not stop everyone from venturing into the lake, however, and on July 6, 1974 a twenty-year-old man named Ronald Westley disappeared while taking a nighttime swim. Forest Preserve police discovered his body the next day.[8]

The water in Maple Lake hasn't been the only danger to visitors. Several horrific crimes have been committed in the surrounding woods, a number of them almost unspeakable. The 1950s were supposed to have been a time of safety, clean lawns, and green bean casserole, but as we have already seen with the murder of the Grimes sisters, that wasn't always the case. In 1955, Maple Lake was the scene of several sex attacks involving three girls—ages eleven, four, and six. Police originally arrested a young man of eighteen years of age named Krause, who one of the victims identified as the perpetrator. At the same time, a Joliet man was arrested in Waukesha, Wisconsin, for tying an eleven-year-old girl to a tree and raping her. After several days, the Joliet man confessed to the crimes near Maple Lake. "It now seems possible that the girl who identified Krause was mistaken," the captain of the Bedford Park Sheriff's Department told the *Daily Tribune*. The case rested on a pair of buckled shoes, which the girls identified the attacker as having worn and which Krause denied ever owning. The man who confessed to the crimes, however, was wearing buckled shoes when he was arrested in Wisconsin. It was a case of mistaken identity, but justice was finally served.[9]

Three years later, in a bizarre and gruesome incident that ended in a shallow grave in the shade of the sugar maples, a young mother alleged that her husband had fathered a baby boy with another woman, brought the child home, and asked her to take care of him. On one morning in March, the husband found the baby dead. The family waited two days before they took the body of the five month old to Maple Lake and buried him in the woods. Police searched for both the grave and the woman's husband, but neither was immediately located.[10] The *Daily Tribune* failed to follow up on the story, so it is unknown whether the husband or the remains of the baby were ever found.

Decades passed before there were any more incidences involving deaths around Maple Lake, but homicide struck twice during the 1990s. Early in April 1991, the body of a teenage girl was found floating in the lake. She "appeared to have been beaten about the face," a detective for the Cook County Forest Preserve District told the *Chicago Tribune*. Less than a day later, police arrested the girl's boyfriend of two years and charged him with her murder.[11] In the fall of 1999, passersby discovered the body of a man in the bushes near the lake. An autopsy determined that he had been killed from a blow to the head. The victim was never identified.[12]

During the 1960s and '70s, Chicago forest preserves developed a bad reputation for crime, drugs, even rumors of black magic, and the woods around Maple Lake were not immune. In the summers of 1967, 1969, and 1977, riots broke out between gangs of youths in the picnic areas of Maple Lake and the Palos Hills Division of the Park District. "Fights Break up Picnics in Suburban Parks," the headlines screamed. "Thousands of Memorial day picnickers were driven from south suburban forest preserves yesterday by roving bands of young toughs."[13]

Although the police claimed that the fighting was not racially motivated, over 100 teens and young adults, both black and white, fought each other near the lake on Memorial Day in 1967. Their weapons included baseball bats, rocks, beer bottles, and even tree branches. It took 200 sheriff's deputies, Chicago police, and forest rangers to restore order. "They scattered pretty quickly when they saw the dog," a deputy told the *Tribune* after he broke up a large group of rioters. Police arrested twenty-nine individuals, ranging in age from eighteen to twenty-two.[14] Two years later, the gangs were back, this time attacking African-Americans picnicking in Maple Lake Woods. One of the injured told the police that "six white youths walked up to his car, blocked it, and swung at it with bats and a crowbar." Despite the large number of perpetrators, police were only able to arrest five, two of them as they attempted to flee the scene in their car.[15] In a similar brawl in 1977, a man was shot in the back of the head and severely wounded. That incident involved around eighty rioters and led to the closing of six picnic groves around the lake.[16] Police threw up their hands in frustration. Willow Springs Police Chief Michael Corbitt told the *Chicago Tribune* that the Palos Division of the Park District was a "Total disaster." "Families cannot go into these woods," he lamented. "They're not secure. The facilities are in disarray. Kids using drugs have taken them over, and nothing is done about it."[17] Thankfully, the situation has improved in the decades since the riots. Hundreds of thousands of visitors come to Maple Lake every year, and the overwhelming majority enjoy themselves in safety.

Strange Lights

If these disturbing events weren't enough to tarnish the reputation of the lake, stories of strange lights have circulated for decades. "An inexplicable red glow has been seen oozing around the shoreline, between the trees and above the sand," *Tribune* reporter Howard Reich wrote in a feature story on Halloween 1980. "The cosmic light rays have defied explanation, since no other similar light source exists for miles around."[18] This "oozing" glow was later described as small and was said to hover in the one particular location in the middle of the lake. The explanation for this light varies from the ghost of a fisherman holding a lantern aloft while he searches for his missing head, to some kind of natural phenomenon.

According to most contemporary accounts, the spook light is most often visible from the Maple Lake Overlook along 95th Street between 10:30pm and 12am, and Dale Kaczmarek reported that it has been seen there since at least the 1950s. Onlookers report that the red light shines brightly for a few precious moments before it disappears. "Average sightings last from a few seconds to about a minute or two with long periods of inactivity," Kaczmarek explained.[19] Richard Crowe had a different experience, however. In *Chicago's Street Guide to the Supernatural*, he claimed that, in 1986, a friend and he witnessed the mysterious light for a much longer period of time. "As we got to the overlook," he wrote, "the red light was there in the distance, bright and burning away. We sat fixated on the sight for a half-hour that night..."[20]

Scientists classify spook lights like the one seen at Maple Lake as *Nocturnal Lights*. More specifically, it is a subtype called a *Ghost Light*. "These are lights, generally spherical, almost always moving just above ground, sometimes disappearing upon approach and reappearing nearby," William Corliss explained in his book *Handbook of Unusual Natural Phenomena*.[21] *Ghost Lights* are tied to a particular location and have localized names. They are distinct from *Will-O'-the-Wisps* and *Natural Flames* because they do not move over long distances and are not obviously caused by escaping gasses. Oftentimes, *Ghost Lights* are caused by the reflection of train or automobile headlights, but every author of Chicago ghostlore agrees that it is unlikely the Maple Lake light has a human or mechanical origin.

As of yet, all of the accounts of the Maple Lake spook light have come from eyewitnesses who happened to be in the right place at the right time. On most pleasant evenings, handfuls of people risk being ticketed by the park rangers to catch a glimpse of this mysterious light, but to my knowledge no one has yet to capture it on film, digital or otherwise. It would be interesting to find out whether the light appears in the absence of a human observer. If it is indeed a natural phenomenon, then it should manifest itself whether there is someone to see it or not. If, on the other hand, the light exists only in the mind of its viewers, then no mechanical instrument will ever capture or measure it. As for its origins, the jury is still out, but the history of Maple Lake certainly has enough fodder to keep the imaginations of storytellers stirring for years to come.

Chapter Endnotes

[1]See: National Park Service, "Illinois & Michigan Canal National Heritage Corridor," http://www.nps.gov/ilmi/.

[2]Troy Taylor, *Haunted Illinois: The Travel Guide to the History & Hauntings of the Prairie State* (Alton: Whitechapel Productions Press, 2004), 264-265.

[3]Dale Kaczmarek, *Windy City Ghosts: An Essential Guide to the Haunted History of Chicago* (Oak Lawn: Ghost Research Society Press, 2005), 100.

[4]*Daily Tribune* (Chicago) 16 June 1930.

[5]*Daily Tribune* (Chicago) 29 June 1934.

[6]*Daily Tribune* (Chicago) 26 July 1934.

[7]*Daily Tribune* (Chicago) 14 June 1936.

[8]*Chicago Tribune* (Chicago) 7 July 1974.

[9]*Daily Tribune* (Chicago) 23 September 1955; *Daily Tribune* (Chicago) 25 September 1955.

[10]*Daily Tribune* (Chicago) 2 May 1958.

[11]*Chicago Tribune* (Chicago) 4 April 1991; *Chicago Tribune* (Chicago) 5 April 1991.

[12]*Chicago Tribune* (Chicago) 21 September 1999.

[13]*Chicago Tribune* (Chicago) 31 May 1967.

[14]*Ibid.*

[15]*Chicago Tribune* (Chicago) 31 May 1969.

[16]*Chicago Tribune* (Chicago) 31 May 1977.

[17]*Chicago Tribune* (Chicago) 19 August 1979.

[18]*Chicago Tribune* (Chicago) 31 October 1980.

[19]Dale Kaczmarek, *Illuminating the Darkness: The Mystery of Spook Lights* (Oak Lawn: Ghost Research Society Press, 2003), 32.

[20]Richard T. Crowe, *Chicago's Street Guide to the Supernatural* (Oak Park: Carolando Press, 2000, 2001), 237.

[21]William R. Corliss, *Handbook of Unusual Natural Phenomena: Eyewitness Accounts of Nature's Greatest Mysteries* (New York: Arlington House, 1986), 68.

St. James-Sag
the "Monk's Castle"

St. James of the Sag Church and Cemetery is the terminus point of the Archer Avenue "triangle." The oldest site of Catholic worship in the county; it sits at the convergence of the Sanitary and Ship Canal and the Calumet Sag Channel, overlooking the Sag Bridge. Route 171 and Route 83 also meet at this point. The church, with its yellow, limestone edifice and adjacent graveyard that spills down a sloping hill, is an impressive sight. Even without the stories, visitors can imagine something otherworldly about this place. Add some lighting and thunder and it could easily be the setting of an Ambrose Bierce novel.

In fact, St. James-Sag was the setting for the area's first Victorian Gothic tale—a ghostly encounter two musicians related to the *Chicago Daily* in 1897 that very well may have been the precursor to two of the most famous of Archer Avenue's folktales: Resurrection Mary and the phantom hearse. The church and cemetery have more than one story to offer, however. For decades eyewitnesses have reported seeing brown robed monks roaming the parish grounds, although the Archdiocese has never stationed any monks there. That particular story has led some locals to dub the church "Monk's Castle."

Although local historians have established some facts about the history of St. James-Sag, most of its past has been obscured by the passage of time, including the origin of the church itself. The church cornerstone reads 1833, but the current building wasn't constructed until 1852. Before that, services were held in a wooden structure, which was a log cabin formerly owned by the Ford family at the bottom of the hill.[1] A century earlier, the hill was the site of a French fort where Catholic missionaries preached to a village of Saganashkee Indians, named after the nearby marshland. Burials at the location date back to the 1830s, although the presence of the French garrison in the 1700s guaranteed that some interments must have taken place there much earlier.[2] The first recorded burial was of a child named Hannah Ford in 1837.[3]

In 1858 the Murphys and the Sullivans, two Irish families who owned nearby land, gave eight acres to the St. James parish for the expressed purpose of a free graveyard. "A clause was inserted, at the dictation of Mrs. Murphy, that any poor man might bury his dead in it without cost," the *Chicago Daily* reported. It was the only cemetery of its kind. The cemetery's first official gravedigger was a Frenchman named John Markex, who, according to legend, didn't know how to dig a grave. His wife, whose father had been a sexton in the old country, took a spade and tutored him. "After that John dug all the graves, when the mourners cared to pay, until it came time for someone else to dig a grave for him."[4] It was understood that only baptized Catholics could be buried in the cemetery proper, and the northwest corner was reserved for non-Catholics and victims of suicide.

St. James-Sag, like the rest of the area, entered a rough period during the 1960s and '70s. In the summer of 1965, vandals looted the church and ran off with gold chalices and other valuables. They caused around $1,000 in damage to the building by breaking a window and tearing the altar cloth. "Father Plozynski said it is the first time in the 132-year history of the church that it had been burglarized," the *Tribune* reported.[5] Vandals struck again in 1969. They tipped headstones, stole the priest's robes, and broke windows. The church became such a target that Bedford Park police put together a special six man taskforce to patrol the grounds. "It's getting so we can't afford our popularity," Father Plozynski lamented.[6]

In the mid-1980s, the Archdiocese of Chicago took over maintenance of the cemetery and decided to modernize its care, which meant that a lot of the character of the graveyard was to be ironed out. For over a hundred years parishioners buried their loved ones as they pleased, therefore the cemetery was laid out in a hap-hazard way that was a nightmare for modern grounds keeping equipment. The Archdiocese's first act was to remove a Tree of Heaven that grew next to the church, and they planned to sod over sunken monuments and smooth the landscape to ease the passage of mowers. Parishioners begged Cardinal Bernardin to retain the original character of the cemetery, but, he replied, the new administrator "is also responsible for maintaining the cemetery in a proper and dignified manner with modern equipment, which was not envisioned 140 years ago..."[7]

In 1984, St. James-Sag Church and Cemetery was added to the National Register of Historic Places. On March 27, 1991, a tornado touched down on the hill and damaged the church's roof. The immediate damage was repaired, but locals soon organized to preserve the site and renovate the 143-year old building. "Church funds barely kept pace with the upkeep of the drafty old building," Michele Mohr wrote in a *Chicago Tribune* special report. "An antiquated boiler system hardly warmed the church, the original pews were worn and pealing, and the outer doors rotted on their hinges." The St. James at Sag Bridge Preservation Society raised several hundred thousand dollars for the repairs.[8]

St. James of the Sag.

Vandalism dogged the cemetery. In 2003, an unknown number of persons climbed the fence and overturned thirty headstones. According to the *Tribune*, church leaders blamed "vandals from teenagers and Goth-types to Satanic cult members obsessed with the lore of the cemetery."[9] The vandals were back six months later, tipping dozens more stones, leading the parish to offer a $500 reward for information leading to the capture of the perpetrators. A number of the damaged monuments, made of limestone, were over a hundred years old.[10] Luckily, in recent years, there have been no more instances of destruction and defacement.

Ghostly Romantic

As alluded to earlier, St. James-Sag was the setting of the area's first ghost story—a romantic tale that involved the specter of a woman in a long, white dress. In *Chicago Haunts*, Ursula Bielski was the first to revive this nearly-forgotten tale, but I went back and read the original 112-year-old article in the *Chicago Daily* in the hopes that it would yield new details. The story, generally, proceeds like this:

> Father Bollman, the priest at St. James, had recently held a church fair at a dance hall located at the bottom of the hill, in the shadow of the parish. The priest hired two musicians; Professor William Looney, a violinist, and John Kelly, a harp player. After the conclusion of the fair, Looney and Kelly settled down for the evening on two cots in the upper floor of the dance hall. At around one o'clock in the morning, Professor Looney awoke to hear the sound of horses and the rumbling wheels of a carriage. The noise passed beneath the window without any sign of horses or carriage. Looney woke Kelly, and at that time the two witnessed an incredible scene. A woman, dressed all in white, appeared in the middle of the road, then proceeded to pass through a fence onto the parish grounds. Moments later, a dark carriage appeared, led by a team of driverless, white horses. The mysterious woman and the carriage then vanished but returned a short time later. The scene repeated itself and the musicians—having seen enough—bolted from the dance hall to the nearby police station.

The *Chicago Daily* reporter described the woman in white as "tall" and added that "her raven black hair hung down her shoulders in tangled confusion… Deep melancholy was reflected from sepulchral eyes which rolled about with that hollow intensity indicative of some soul-eating despair." Amusingly, the reporter also wrote, "the young woman was agile beyond the hopes of the most ardent flying machine enthusiast." The illustration that accompanied the article depicted the young ghost as possessing blonde, or at least light colored, hair. The riderless carriage bore an uncanny resemblance to the legendary hearse mentioned in our chapter on Archer Woods Cemetery. "Snow white horses covered with fine netting" drove the carriage described by William Looney and John Kelly. Most similarly, "A light of electric brilliancy shone from the forehead of each." These two lights resembled the gas lanterns that hung from the phantom hearse, as did the character of the horses, which were "high-strung and came with frantic speed."[11]

Was that ghostly encounter the long-lost inspiration for the stories of Resurrection Mary and the terrifying phantom hearse? Ken O'Brien of the *Chicago Tribune* didn't think so. He claimed the story was rooted in a different tradition. According to "old-timers," a young man and woman who worked at St. James-Sag church in the 1880s fell in love and decided to elope. "The boy hitched horses to a wagon and told her to wait halfway down the hill," O'Brien wrote. "When he approached, she yelled, 'Come on,' and hopped aboard. But the horses bolted, overturning the wagon and killing them."[12] Despite the popularity of the story, there are no accounts of the ghosts other than that given by Looney and Kelly, but Ursula Bielski suggested that in the years after the story was lost, the memory of the forlorn woman in white and the black carriage survived, taking form further north along Archer Avenue. "The modernized legend of Resurrection Mary simply accounts for too many of the elements of the elopement legend of St. James-Sag," she wrote. Along with the previously mentioned similarities, Bielski added, "Some old accounts of Resurrection Mary claim that the dance attended by this young woman was, in fact, a church dance, perhaps the folkloric version of the dance hall church fair where Looney and Kelly were playing."[13]

Phantom Monks

The other folktale associated with St. James-Sag concerns phantom monks that have been spotted roaming the hillside, giving rise to the name "Monk's Castle." The monks struck terror in the hearts of anyone who dared to violate the sanctuary of the church. There was a rumor among local youth, no doubt brought on by exaggerated stories of discipline at the area's parochial schools, that the monks would force anyone unlucky enough to be caught inside the cemetery gates after dark to kneel on ball bearings. According to Dale Kaczmarek, Father George Aschenbremer, one of the parish priests during the 1970s, chased trespassers away using a bullhorn and a flashlight. His real-life activities spawned stories that a "mad monk" dwelled in the rectory.[14]

In 1977, a police officer named Roberts had an encounter with the phantom monks. Because of vandalism at the church, police regularly stopped at St. James-Sag to make sure all was well. On that particular evening, Richard Crowe retold, "As Roberts pulled up in front of St. James Sag's massive front gates that had been locked for the night, he noticed some figures moving about inside." There were as many as nine, walking in single file. The officer yelled at them to stop, then when they did not, he grabbed his shotgun and gave chase. The hooded figures seemed to vanish, however, when they reached the church. Roberts omitted some of these details from his official report, but he later confided in Mr. Crowe the most hair raising aspects of the incident.[15]

According to Trent Brandon's *Book of Ghosts*, the phantom monks of St. James-Sag belong to a type of ghost he calls "The Spiritual Specter." These are the ghosts of priests, monks, nuns, and other members of religious orders who haunt their earthly habitats long after they pass away. They are usually benevolent. "Spiritual specters do not let death stop them from continuing their holy work and from helping people," Brandon explained.[16] Are the phantom monks of St. James-Sag protecting the parish from harm? After years of vandalism and a tornado strike, that wouldn't appear to be the case. Additionally, no members of a religious order were ever stationed there. These robed figures appear to be the result of either overactive imaginations, or something more real and sinister. If what officer Roberts saw were not ghosts but living persons, however, what were they doing there? As Dale Kaczmarek speculated, "Perhaps some of these figures were not spirits at all but a nearby group of Satanists."[17]

Standing in the shadow of St. James-Sag, with all its rich history, it is easy to let your imagination get the better of you. The stories of phantom monks contain a grab bag of Catholic stereotypes and assumptions about the mystical aspects of the faith, and more than likely belong to the realm of folklore and fiction. No one has ever seen the monks in the daylight, and it would be easy to lose several figures along the sloping ground of St. James-Sag in the darkness of night. Furthermore, the hooded sweatshirt of a trespasser might easily be mistaken for a monk's robe if stories have preconditioned an eyewitness to believe that's what he or she will encounter.

Nevertheless, there is no mistaking that St. James of the Sag Church and Cemetery is the anchor for the paranormal phenomenon rumored to lurk along this stretch of Route 171. While plenty of Chicago area churches lay claim to being haunted, St. James-Sag is the only one to inhabit such a prominent position on the landscape, both physical as well as metaphysical. In its nearly two centuries overlooking the Des Plaines and Sag valleys, it has earned a permanent and nefarious place in the folk history of Archer Avenue.

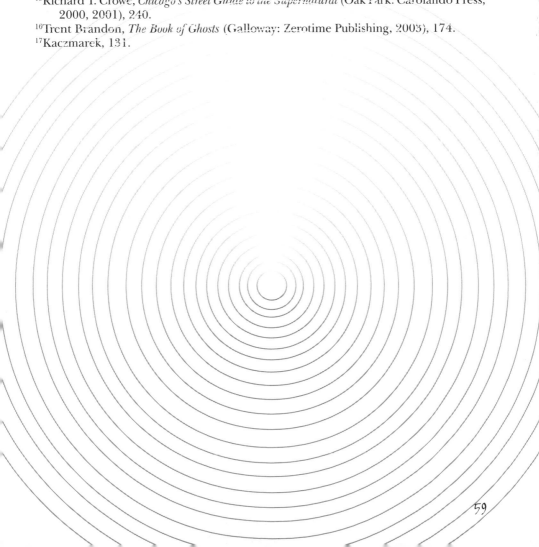

Chapter Endnotes

[1]*Chicago Tribune* (Chicago) 17 June 1986.
[2]*Daily Tribune* (Chicago) 20 September 1956.
[3]*Chicago Tribune* (Chicago) 12 May 1996.
[4]*Chicago Daily* (Chicago) 12 September 1897.
[5]*Chicago Tribune* (Chicago) 5 June 1965.
[6]*Chicago Tribune* (Chicago) 12 November 1969.
[7]*Chicago Tribune* (Chicago) 17 June 1986.
[8]*Chicago Tribune* (Chicago) 12 May 1996.
[9]*Chicago Tribune* (Chicago) 7 June 2003.
[10]*Chicago Tribune* (Chicago) 6 December 2003.
[11]*Chicago Daily* (Chicago) 20 September 1897.
[12]*Chicago Tribune* (Chicago) 7 March 1999.
[13]Ursula Bielski, *Chicago Haunts: Ghostlore of the Windy City* (Chicago: Lake Claremont Press, 1998), 79-80.
[14]Dale Kaczmarek, *Windy City Ghosts: An Essential Guide to the Haunted History of Chicago* (Oak Lawn: Ghost Research Society Press, 2005), 130.
[15]Richard T. Crowe, *Chicago's Street Guide to the Supernatural* (Oak Park: Carolando Press, 2000, 2001), 240.
[16]Trent Brandon, *The Book of Ghosts* (Galloway: Zerotime Publishing, 2003), 174.
[17]Kaczmarek, 131.

Part 2
Haunted Colleges
&
Universities

Western Illinois University and the Ghosts of Simpkins Hall

Imagine you are a student going off to college for the first time. At home, you gave a sigh of relief as you opened your acceptance letter. Now, you are ready to put childhood behind you as you tuck your English lit textbook under your arm and enter one of the three arched doorways to Simpkins Hall, a stark, neoclassical building rising four stories with rows of windows cut along its face. Your footsteps echo in the foyer as you climb the stairwell to the first floor. The beige, tiled walls are oddly comforting, but something seems wrong as you scan the empty hallway. Where are the other students? Florescent lights flicker on and off. Without warning, the laughter of a young child echoes down the dark corridor.

For years, students and faculty in Western Illinois University's Simpkins Hall have told similar stories, but the ghost of an adolescent girl—so seemingly out of place—is only one of the apparitions rumored to haunt the seventy-one-year-old building. Many other odd occurrences at the hall are attributed to "Harold," a former janitor or graduate assistant who lurks among the classrooms on the third floor. After classes finish for the day, the disembodied sound of keys jingling, doors opening and closing, or a typewriter clicking, rattle the nerves of even the most seasoned educator. Nevertheless, tales of encounters with the ghost of Harold and the phantom child have made believers of some, but many in this ivory tower remain skeptical.

Nestled in the small town of Macomb, Western Illinois University is somewhat isolated from the rest of the state due to the lack of direct Interstate access. It is located in an area of Illinois known during the 1960s and '70s as "Forgottonia," a tongue and cheek reference to a sixteen-county region of western Illinois long ignored by state legislators. In 1972, a student at WIU proclaimed himself "Governor of Forgottonia" to protest the lack of state funding to the region, and the would-be secessionist named the tiny village of Fandon as its new capital.[1]

Western Illinois University began, like many other universities in the State of Illinois, as a teacher's college. Originally called Western Illinois State Normal School, its classes were confined to one building, now known as Sherman Hall. Sherman Hall was then known by the unimaginative title of "Main Building." In 1902, the university added a training school to Main Building in order to allow its students to obtain teaching experience in the classroom. Local children enrolled in the Training School and were taught by the students at the college. Main Building soon became overcrowded, and like his counterpart at Eastern Illinois State Normal School, the president of Western, Walter P. Morgan, doggedly pursued the addition of a new building for his college.

Finally, in 1937, WIU received a federal grant through the Works Progress Administration, part of President Roosevelt's New Deal, for a new training school on campus. The Jacobson Brothers of Chicago designed the building to resemble a large, rectangular high school like the kind seen in Chicago or New York, complete with ornate carvings above the doors and sculpted lion's heads on the roof.

According to Nicole Banks, who wrote a history of Simpkins Hall for the WIU English Department, the Training School was a self-contained educational unit. The ground floor housed the kindergarten and first grade, as well as the gymnasium, lunchroom, and infirmary. The first floor was devoted to second through fifth grades, as well as the administration offices. Sixth through eighth grades occupied the second floor, and the high school was located on the third floor. The entire building was designed to accommodate around 300 young students.[2]

In the 1960s, as Western Illinois State Normal School became Western Illinois University, the Training School building was converted to house the Department of English and Journalism. All of the children left to make room for the deluge of incoming college freshmen from the baby boom generation, but many reminders of the building's past remained behind. There were closets with tape still bearing the names of the last occupants, rows of green lockers, tiny desks, and wooden loudspeakers. The building appeared eerily similar to the high schools from which its new students had just graduated. Certainly, it would have been easy for them to imagine groups of grade-schoolers being herded down the narrow hallways. With such a unique past, Simpkins Hall, as it was christened in 1968, was a natural incubator for ghost stories.

A Mixed Up Haunting

The ghostly tales in Simpkins Hall have been told since at least the 1980s, but few are in agreement on the details. Every storyteller adds his or her own twist with each retelling. The gender and even the number of adolescent phantoms vary from person to person. For instance, in 2004, Tim Mulcrone, a former student at WIU, wrote, "Simpkins is allegedly haunted by two little girls who drowned in Lake Ruth. Now they run around the building singing, laughing, and climbing the stairs…"[3] Most of the storytellers describe the ghost as a young girl, but *Western Courier*

Simpkins Hall at
Western Illinois University

reporter Sarah Cash uncovered the story of a boy who drowned in Lake Ruth, a pond directly south of Simpkins Hall. That incident could have been the historic origin of the legend. A composition instructor named Penny Rigg told Miss Cash that she had heard about the drowning from a former student who graduated from WIU in either 1938 or 1944. According to the former student, the young boy drowned in the lake during a picnic. He was unconscious when the picnickers pulled him onto dry land, and for some unexplained reason, they brought him to the fourth floor of Simpkins Hall. He supposedly died in the former Training School library, which is now the Writing Center.[4]

Harold

The other eerie inhabitant of Simpkins is the ghost of a former student or employee affectionately named "Harold." Harold is fingered as the origin of every strange sound and happening on the third floor and in the fourth floor Writing Center. Compared to the phantom child, Harold is a relatively recent ghost. Randy Smith and Judi Hardin, who have both been at the university for decades, told *Western Courier* reporter Sarah Cash that they first heard the Harold stories in the 1980s. Miss Cash believed the story might have its origins in the experience of a former teaching assistant named C.K. Bryant, who heard typing early one morning as she lay down to rest her eyes in the Writing Center. Bryant got up to investigate, but the noise stopped. It returned, however, as soon as she lay down again. Exasperated, she yelled, "Harold, knock it off!" She did not hear the mysterious sounds again that morning.

"She was not sure why she used the name Harold, but it had worked," Cash concluded.

Another teaching assistant told the reporter that she had returned from getting a soda from the vending machine one evening to find a mysterious message on her word processor. The window with her paper on it had been minimized and replaced with one containing random characters and the word "hi." The Writing Center door had been locked while three other students and she went to the vending machine.[5] These experiences have led to Harold being called the "typing ghost."

A Human Comedy

One more rumor circulating the hall is that of a woman crying in the first floor restroom.[6] This story seems to have come about in recent years, and might have more to do with the condition of the facilities than anything paranormal. As Eddie Rybarski humorously wrote in the

Western Courier, "The fear is not about hearing 'boo!' but, while subjected to the child-sized stalls, being 'peek-a-booed.'"[7]

Still, many remain skeptical. "I have heard all the stories, but believe none of them," Michael Baumann, a teaching assistant whose office is located at the center of the ghostly rumors, told me. "It's a large old building that serves hundreds of people each day. Weird noises and things like that do happen, but given the size and multiple uses of the building, one is never alone in Simpkins. With the theater department embedded within the inner core of the building, it's not surprising that people claim to hear ghosts. I've heard that there is a typing ghost in my office, and after a year I haven't heard anything beside rain hitting the tiled roof."[8] James Courter, an instructor at WIU, agreed. "I have no encounters with ghosts in Simpkins Hall to report, nor do I believe any of the stories that have circulated over the years," he said. "However, I can't resist responding to your question about whether I have ever experienced anything 'out of the ordinary' there. WIU's English Department… has a long and rich history of out-of-the-ordinary behavior, all of it based on human nature and a menagerie of characters with conflicting wills, ambitions, politics and worldviews. It is, in short, an excellent window on The Human Comedy, no ghosts required."[9] Most of the professors and teaching assistants with whom I corresponded denied having ever seen or heard anything unusual in the hall.

The only book of ghostlore to mention Simpkins Hall, aside from my own, was *Haunted Places: The National Directory* by Dennis William Hauck,[10] but the building has attracted more attention in recent years. In September 2003, a psychic and paranormal investigator named Gary Hawkins visited Western and held a ghost hunting workshop complete with lessons in the use of electromagnetic field detectors and dowsing rods. Students paid $25 for the two hour session. Among his wilder claims, such as the ability to catch ghosts with his bare hands, Mr. Hawkins alleged to have contacted the ghost of an eight year old boy in Simpkins Hall. With a touch of skepticism, *Western Courier* reporter David Fitzgerald wrote, "He [Hawkins] added that professors in the building had experienced 'things' that corroborated his findings."[11] I recently wrote to Mr. Hawkins, and he elaborated on his experience at Western. Although it had been six years, his recollection of his own encounter with the ghost was sharp in his mind. "There was no actual communication with the boy, he did not say anything," he explained. "I sensed he was there, his age, and obviously that he was a male child. He mainly stayed in one room of the hall. If memory serves me correctly, it was on the first floor. That night he was mainly trying to stay out of the way, while curious as to what we were doing."[12]

More paranormal investigators followed. In the spring of 2008, a tour company called "A Midwest Haunting" got permission from university administrators to conduct tours of Simpkins Hall. Co-owners Tim Weaver and Chad Frederick brought various "ghost hunting" equipment on the tours and invited their guests to participate in an investigation of the hall. "A Midwest Haunting will… provide the building's historical background to participants and will teach them what to look for as they are guided around the building," the *Macomb Eagle* reported.[13] On one tour session, a man captured a blurry image on his digital camera in a stairwell, eliciting gasps of excitement. "Everyone here is ready for some suspension of disbelief," wrote *Daily Herald* reporter Jonathan Jacobson, who witnessed the events that night. There were enough scares to go around. One young woman was shaken up when she felt something grab her leg.[14] "A Midwest Haunting" ran at WIU every weekend from March 21 to April 12.

Despite the disbelief of many of the staff working in Simpkins Hall, Mr. Weaver insists that his tour participants experienced paranormal activity. "During one of our tours a woman was in the writing center investigating and reported [that] a chair moved against the door trapping her inside," he told me. "Also on the northeast stairs by the rehearsal hall we received heavy EMF readings and caught a picture of a small girl tugging on a lady taking the tour. This can be seen on our Facebook group… Another lady felt a tug on her sleeve in a stairwell leading to the basement and passed out." EMF is short for Electromagnetic Field. An electromagnetic field is one of the four forces of nature and is produced by electrically charged objects. Radio waves, light waves, infrared, and microwaves are all examples of electromagnetic fields. It would not be out of the ordinary for an EMF meter to detect the waves inside a building, where sources of electricity are abundant. Nevertheless, some people believe EMF meters alert them to the presence of ghosts.

"When we run a ghost tour in a building we put a considerable amount of research and investigation into it before it is available to the public," Mr. Weaver added. "Hundreds of people over the years have reported the same stories of Simpkins Hall."[15]

More WIU Hauntings

But Simpkins is not the only building at Western Illinois University rumored to be haunted. Thanks to the widespread availability of the Internet on college campuses, every unexplained experience can be broadcast around the world, and stories that used to take decades to see the light of day now explode into the public consciousness in weeks or even days. In addition to being transmitted orally, stories are simply copied-and-pasted onto multiple websites and discussion boards. Sometimes the author will add experiences of his or her own. It was in this manner that the other hauntings at WIU came to my attention. According to these (usually) anonymous postings, Bayliss, Tanner, Thompson, and Washington Halls all have their own ghosts. The four are residence halls, so it is not surprising that unusual tales have flourished there.

Bayliss Hall is allegedly haunted by the ghosts of two suicide victims. In the first story, a freshman girl became pregnant while away at school and delivered the baby in her dorm room, afraid of what her parents would do if they found out. In a panic, the girl threw the baby—along with any evidence of the delivery—down the garbage chute. She then hung herself in the closet. Some students claim that the cries of both the girl and the baby echo through the hall. In the second story, the room-mate of a young woman suffering from severe depression left her alone over the weekend, and like in the aforementioned story, the depressed girl ended her life in the closet. The girl's roommate discovered her body upon returning Sunday evening. Today, residents of that particular room report strange noises and electrical disturbances.

In Tanner Hall, the ghost of a young man who met his fate during a water fight is said to haunt the twelfth floor. Sadly, this particular student dove into the elevator shaft and fell to his death. The incident alleg-edly occurred in 1972. Students also report hearing strange banging and knocking sounds around one particular room in Thompson Hall. In Washington Hall, a girl supposedly ended her life after a fight with her boyfriend. According to the storytellers, the phone in her former room rings and no one is on the line. The contributor of this particular posting added that the girl's parents tried to cover up the suicide by claiming she died from diabetes.[16]

Unlike the ghost stories in Simpkins Hall, four of the five dormroom tales deal with anxiety-provoking issues for college students. We know that student suicides and incidents of mothers discarding their newborn babies into the trash are all too real. These occurrences may be extremely rare, but this type of ghostlore reminds students of their fears. The tale of the roommate's suicide in Bayliss Hall serves as a dramatic morality play, warning students to look after their fellow classmates. There are clear lessons in all of these stories, and without explicitly stating it, they hammer home the point in a way that is likely to stick with both story-teller and his or her audience. They are even more prescient because, sadly, there really are suicides on college campuses across the country, although the majority of the victims are male. In the case of Western Illinois University's residence halls, even though each tale may not be rooted in a specific incident, they illuminate harsh realities lurking be-neath an otherwise care-free campus life. In 1990, a freshman student did pass away in WIU's Henninger Hall, although he died of alcohol poisoning, not suicide.[17] Sadly, such events are the dark underside to the culture at our universities, a culture that is reflected in contempo-rary campus folklore.

Chapter Endnotes

[1]James D. Nowlan, "From Lincoln to Forgottonia," *Illinois Issues* 24 (September 1998): 27-30.

[2]Nicole Banks, "Simpkins Hall History," *Western Illinois University Department of English & Journalism*, <http://www.wiu.edu/english/simpkins/history.shtml> (13 May 2009).

[3]*Western Courier* (Macomb) 7 April 2004.

[4]*Western Courier* (Macomb) 31 October 2007.

[5]*Ibid.*

[6]*Macomb Eagle* (Macomb) 15 February 2008.

[7]*Western Courier* (Macomb) 21 March 2008.

[8]Michael Baumann, "Re: ghosts in simpkins hall," personal email (16 May 2009).

[9]James E. Courter, "Re: Ghosts in Simpkins Hall," personal email (19 May 2009).

[10]Dennis William Hauck, *Haunted Places: The National Directory: Ghostly Abodes, Sacred Sites, UFO Landings, and Other Supernatural Locations* (New York: Penguin Books, 1994, 1996), 161.

[11]*Western Courier* (Macomb) 8 September 2003.

[12]Gary S. Hawkins, "Re: Ghost in Simpkins Hall," personal email (19 May 2009).

[13]*Macomb Eagle* (Macomb) 15 February 2008.

[14]*Daily Herald* (Arlington Heights) 4 April 2008.

[15]Tim E. Weaver, "Re: Hauntings at WIU," personal email (18 May 2009).

[16]Lorenashley, "Ghost stories from my lil college town," 10 May 2007, <http://teamsugar.com/250490> (2 May 2009).

[17]*Western Courier* (Macomb) 24 October 1990.

Rockford College

The third largest city in Illinois, Rockford was established as a blue-collar town along the Rock River less than twenty miles from the Wisconsin border. Often overshadowed by the Chicago metropolitan area to the east, Rockford, with its estimated 168,000 residents, has made its own contributions to our great state. While the city is known as a manufacturing hub, it is also home to several colleges. Rockford's first college, established before the city was even chartered, was Rockford Female Seminary. Jane Addams, who would go on to fame as a social reformer and co-founder of Chicago's Hull House, was a graduate of the seminary in 1881. In 1892, RFS became known as Rockford College, which remained a predominately female academy until 1958. In 1964, the campus was moved from its home along the river to its present location along State Street.

While rich in history, Rockford College is also rich in ghostlore and the origin of a wide variety of alleged haunts. No less than three buildings are said to be home to restless spirits, along with one memorial arch, which was built using materials from the original Rock River campus. Blanche Walker Burpee Center, Adams Arch, Clark Arts Center, and McGaw Residence Hall run the gambit of ghostly phenomenon, from disembodied voices, to moving objects, to phantom reflections, and a whole host of other unexplained things. In October 2008, Kathi Kresol, a local librarian, conducted a tour group through campus. For the past five years Kathi has run tours of haunted places in Rockford around Halloween as a special event associated with the Rockford Public Library.

Clark Arts Center

Out of all of the buildings at Rockford College, the Clark Arts Center, which contains both Cheek and Maddox theaters, is thought to be the most haunted. That should not come as a surprise, since many theaters are believed to have their own resident ghosts. A great deal of emotion is poured out on stage at rehearsals and performances, in love affairs and personality clashes between cast and crew. Theaters are therefore saturated with emotional energy, even long after the lights go off. The Clark Arts Center is no exception, and may even be more active than most. It is generally believed to be haunted by a former Theater Arts professor named Knox Fowler, who designed the building in 1971 and died of cancer shortly thereafter. Many of the flickering lights and strange noises are blamed on his ghost.

Maddox Theatre

The arts center is an impressive building. Inside a second floor entrance stands a statue of a horse—made from petrified wood. It is eerily skeletal and lifelike. Ancient frescos depicting figures in various stages of celebration, often playing instruments, line the hall outside Maddox Theatre. Their cherubic faces, it has been said, change expressions and even watch the audience as the guests filter in for a performance. Aboriginal artifacts from Africa, as well as a collection of Hopi Indian kachina dolls, are also on display in the hallways that lead to the class and practice rooms. In the traditional Hopi religion, kachina dolls are thought to embody a variety of spirits. For many years, these fragile bowls, masks, and dolls were locked in a storage room. No one ever entered there alone. Visitors often reported a heavy, ominous feeling, as though the artifacts were somehow hostile to their presence. Building service workers refused to clean the room, and eventually the artifacts were removed and placed where they are currently on display.[1]

Maddox Theatre is the largest of the two in Clark Arts Center, and possesses an atmosphere all its own. Mannequins donned in Shakespearian dress stand on platforms above the ornately-carpeted foyer outside the auditorium, while chandeliers hang from the ceiling. Behind the stage, in the dressing rooms, students have reported that lights flicker with no probable cause. According to Haunted Rockford, a website devoted to haunted places in the Rockford metropolitan area, some visitors have heard loud screaming after everyone else has gone home. In the prop room, a bell supposedly rings on its own. The explanation behind the strange behavior of the bell was that an actress, who was very sick, used it to call for help, but she died several days later. Another auditory phenomenon described by students involved a tapping sound that has been heard after the lights were turned off.[2] In *Haunted Illinois*, Troy Taylor added that, "there have been reports of flickering lights, piano music and footsteps on the catwalks above the stage."[3] When Kathi Kresol brought her tour group into the theater, one young woman smelled lilac perfume.[4]

Cheek Theatre

Cheek Theatre, named after Mary Ashby Cheek, is a much smaller theater located on the ground floor opposite of Maddox. It has very limited seating and serves as a practice stage for future thespians. The walls are painted black, giving it a gloomy appearance that compliments its resident ghost. Before some performances, theater students say they have seen a shadowy figure. They assert the figure is the ghost of a former music teacher who died in a car accident. Ms. Kresol invited a psychic, Mark Dorsett, to participate in her tour of Rockford College. He claimed to have gotten an "impression" of the ghost during his visit. "[There is a] younger male who felt more like a professor, I was guessing around 30 or so," he told her. "[The ghost] really is a gifted musician and just like the crew and cast have heard, he gets stressed before a performance and paces and plays to calm himself."[5]

Adams Arch

A few yards south of the Clark Arts Center rests a scenic memorial known as Adams Arch. As a remnant of the original campus along the Rock River, the arch is said to contain within it a little more of the past than its donors intended. It formerly served as the doorway to Adams Hall, which was built in 1891. After Rockford College moved in 1964, a generous family thought at least part of the old campus should be preserved. The result was a beautiful marble and stone structure, ornately carved with two small stained glass windows. A plaque on the arch reads, in part, "The initial disassembly and subsequent reconstruction in 1975 were done by Gust G. Larson and sons to memorialize the parents of the principals in that organization."

It was dedicated in 2005 to Gust G. Larson, Anna M. Larson, and their son, whose firm built the Burpee Center, Clark Arts Center, and other campus buildings. Since the college was an all-female institution for over a century before moving to its current location, the memorial arch is believed to contain within it—like music recorded on a cassette—the sounds of past female students. On certain evenings, when the air is very still, visitors have reported hearing the laughter of young women in the vicinity of the arch. "That piece of the college's history goes way, way back," Kathi Kresol told the Rockford *Register Star*. "It's one of the oldest things out there. What I've been told is, the laughter isn't one girl or a group of particular girls. It represents all of the girls."[6]

Blanche Walker Burpee Center

About a hundred yards past the main entrance to Rockford College sits the Blanche Walker Burpee Center. The Burpee Center is not the kind of place one would usually associate with phantoms and other denizens of the afterlife. It is a modern, well-lit building that serves as the college's welcome center as well as the bookstore and the offices

Adams Arch, Rockford College.

for administrative services. Some students and storytellers maintain that the basement formerly held a radio station that was the scene of a man's suicide. No one is quite clear about who this man was, whether a student or employee, but individuals who find themselves in the building after hours report hearing doors slamming shut, footsteps, and a man's disembodied voice in the basement. One frequently-repeated story was that an employee was working late in the former radio station and saw a reflection in the window. He turned around to greet the visitor, only to discover that he was still alone. Before he could return to his work, a breeze blew the papers off his desk, revealing an old newspaper article about the man who had committed suicide.[7]

McGaw Residence Hall

While a small college by any standard, Rockford does provide some on-campus student housing. McGaw Residence Hall, the largest of the bunch, is tucked behind a wooded area and has been closed to students for the past several years. Enrollment at Rockford College has declined from its peak in 1994, making McGaw not cost effective to open. There are around 200 less full-time students enrolled today than there were fourteen years ago.[8] The empty dorm has developed its own unusual reputation. Of course, any abandoned building on a college campus is going to accumulate rumors as students struggle to explain why it sits unused. The stories surrounding McGaw Hall, however, come from a time, or times, when it was occupied. Once again, the Internet has played a central role in perpetuating these particular stories, with web contributors adding their own details into the mix.

McGaw Hall is accessible via both a narrow drive and a walking path that wind their way through a wooded area at the extreme northeast corner of the campus. The hall itself is situated on a plateau between a creek and a hill, making it difficult to spot from anywhere else on campus, even though it is over six stories tall. Today, the building's only visitors are birds that nest on its roof, or curious groups of students who come to explore and perhaps cause mischief. The windows are dirty or cracked, and a few are broken and covered with boards. Cigarette butts and old leaves from the previous fall are piled up on the concrete outside the chained doors. A lone pine tree gently sways in the breeze. Beneath this tree sits a discrete memorial to Janey Schell, a young woman whose tragic death in January 1979 spawned one of the most enduring legends at Rockford College. Grace, a friend of Janey's roommate who asked to remain anonymous, was there that night.

"I went back to Barrington for the weekend," she told me. "Liz Haines, also from Barrington, was going to go back with me to visit her parents. At the last minute, she decided to stay on campus. Returning to campus, it was a very warm night, especially for January. The fog was so thick, that cars could only travel about 10 mph, to travel by the middle line, so the trip took much longer than usual. I had just reached my room, and looked out the windows, and saw lights and ambulance headed to the dorm... Had Liz gone home with me, she would have just been getting back, and might not have known where her room-mate was. By staying, Liz was around and talking with Janey, and knew that Janey was going to take a bath. A little unusual, in that there are mainly showers in McGaw. In any case, when Janey did not come back after awhile, and I believe that there was a phone call for [her]—no cell or cordless phones then—Liz went to tell Janey, and found her... in the tub. Autopsy showed that she had died of an epileptic seizure. She had never been diagnosed with epilepsy, and had never had a full incident—until that night. Just one of the awful weekends that began that semester..."[9]

Like James Dallas Egbert III and the campus myth of the "Steam Tunnel Incident," details of Janey's death have been whispered from one generation to next, until it too has become campus lore. According to legend, an epileptic girl was staying in McGaw Hall over Thanksgiving break. Despite being alone, she decided to take a bath. She suffered a seizure in one of the bathtubs and hit her head and drowned because no one was around to help. Some have added other details, for instance that her room was located on the fifth floor, but everyone agrees that her ghost now haunts the hall. According to Troy Taylor, "Female students who use the shower room here often report the eerie sounds of a woman singing and will occasionally find that bath and personal items sometimes disappear from their room."[10] Personal encounters with the ghost have fueled the story. While the building is currently closed to students, it has occasionally hosted visitors for special events. A cheerleading squad stayed on the sixth floor for four days in 2004, and the young women posted some of their experiences on a website, where their encounters with the unseen were then picked up and spread around the World Wide Web. The cheerleaders described hearing a girl singing in the shower and a man's voice even though there were no men in the building. Several young women sleeping in Room 603 said they heard a chair slide across the floor in the room directly above, but no one was staying there and that room was locked. On other occasions, items mysteriously fell off shelves.[11]

With the notable exception of McGaw Hall, there is no evidence that any of the deaths described by the preceding stories actually took place. But the ghost stories at Rockford College persist despite the lack of concrete evidence because their truthfulness is incidental to their purpose. To the students of the college, especially those with a more artistic disposition, it doesn't matter whether or not the stories of sui-cide or accidental death are true. The presence of "ghosts" in Maddox

Theatre, the Burpee Center, or Adams Arch lend a certain sense of uniqueness and continuity to campus life beyond the boring, everyday routine of reading, homework, or sitting in class. As long as students occupy its halls, Rockford College will always remain haunted.

Chapter Endnotes

[1] Kathi Kresol, "Stop #3," Haunted Rockford Tour 2008: 3.

[2] "Rockford College," Haunted Rockford: Bringing the Area's Best Kept Secrets to You, <http://hauntedrockford.webs.com/rockfordcollege.htm> (2 May 2009).

[3] Troy Taylor, Haunted Illinois: The Travel Guide to the History & Hauntings of the Prairie State (Alton: Whitechapel Productions Press, 2004), 243.

[4] Michael Kleen, "Interview with Kathi Kresol," Legends and Lore of Illinois 3 (June 2009): 6.

[5] Mark Dorsett, Psychic Impressions of Mark Dorsett as Given to Kathi Kresol, October 2008, 3.

[6] Register Star (Rockford) 31 October 2008.

[7] Taylor, 243.

[8] Rockford College Factbook (Fall 2008): 4.

[9] Grace [redacted], "Re: question," personal email (22 September 2009).

[10] Taylor, 243.

[11] "Rockford College," Haunted Rockford: Bringing the Area's Best Kept Secrets to You, <http://hauntedrockford.webs.com/rockfordcollege.htm> (2 May 2009).

Illinois State University and the Enduring Legacy of Ange Milner

Jesse W. Fell, a Bloomington newspaper publisher, founded Illinois State Normal University in 1857 with the help of his friend, lawyer and legislator Abraham Lincoln, who would go on to become our sixteenth president. Originally a teacher's college, ISNU became Illinois State University in 1968 to accommodate a broader curriculum. The university is currently home to around 23,000 students and faculty, as well as one tenacious ghost. The ghost is said to be that of Angeline V. Milner, or Ange for short, a beloved librarian who remained with her books long after she passed from this world. Although now often spelled Angie, Angeline is commonly abbreviated in the original French as Ange. In Charles William Perry's 1924 biography of Miss Milner, he omitted the 'i' from the diminutive form of her name.[1] As head librarian for thirty-seven years, she was so beloved by the school that Illinois State University named its library after her.

Angeline Vernon Milner was born on April 9, 1856 in Bloomington, Illinois. She did not often stray from her hometown in her 72 years on this earth, and left an indelible mark on the community. By all accounts, she seemed to be destined for the work which would become her legacy. According to Charles W. Perry, who assisted the famed librarian for several years, she learned how to read before she was four years old. Ange's mother was educated in Boston and kept her home well supplied with books, which a young Ange would organize according to size and color. She was homeschooled for most of her adolescence, then attended a variety of schools. Her frail constitution prevented her from being away from home for very long. She attended Bloomington High School for only one year in 1870-71, left to visit an aunt in Massachusetts, and returned to attend classes sporadically at the high school. She never graduated, which was not unusual at the time. Compulsory education for minors wasn't instituted in Illinois until 1883.

Undaunted, Miss Milner sought to expand her education at the Vacation School of the Illinois State Laboratory of Natural History at Normal University in 1875 and 1878. Around the same time, her love of books led her to organize a club devoted to the study of American literature and to join another group, the Paladin Club, for a similar purpose. When she was twenty-eight, her failing health compelled her to take a break from these activities, and she spent several years looking after her mother, who had also fallen ill. It seemed like nothing would ever change for Ange, until she finally found her calling in a chance opportunity at Normal University.

Ange might never have worked as a librarian if not for her younger sister Laura, who was attending Normal University in the fall of 1889. At the time, many libraries were held by private literary societies. Two such societies decided to donate their collections to Normal University, and the university needed someone to catalogue all the new additions. Laura, being familiar with her sister's passion, insisted that Ange apply for the position. After some trepidation, Ange sent her application to the president of Normal University, but nearly a year went by before she got the news that she had been hired. Miss Milner began her fated job at the university library on February 1, 1890. The Normal School Board was so impressed with her dedication that they appointed her as the sole and head librarian in the fall of that same year.

Despite her growing deafness, Angeline Milner performed her job with an attentiveness rarely seen in civil servants, and her passion for books made her somewhat of a celebrity in the state of Illinois. She helped form the Illinois Library Association in 1896 and became its president in 1907-08. As she was elected to the position, a man named Mr. Roden presented her with a plant on behalf of what he referred to as "the fast vanishing race of men librarians." Miss Milner was also a member of the American Library Association and an honorary member of the Philadelphian Society and the Wrightonian Society. During the First World War, she wrote over 600 letters to servicemen at the front and composed several poems regarding the war.

Ange was intimately familiar with the literary collection at Normal University. In the May 1924 issue of *The Alumni Quarterly*, Charles W. Perry related the story of how a member of the faculty, Mr. Manchester, went to Miss Milner's office in search of a book "not knowing the name of the author, title, color of book, size, shape or anything that would help Miss Milner to identify the book. Miss Milner told him to wait a minute and she went to Mr. Ridgley's office and brought back a book. 'Is this the book you wanted?' Mr. Manchester said that it was."[2] Because of her deafness, Miss Milner received all queries and questions written on pieces of paper. She helped almost everyone with equal passion, but gave a stern lecture to those students who sought out her help right before a deadline. Mr. Perry wrote that Ange corresponded with hundreds of students and offered advice and assistance even after their time at the university was over. Consequently, she left her mark on generations of students, who came to regard her as "Aunt Ange."

Mr. Perry described her as being of below average height, with a slender build and soft white hair. She possessed boundless energy, a sharp memory, and was a bit of a pack rat, keeping everything she thought might be useful to someone at some time in the future. From Perry's description, it seemed the ill health of her youth left her in the autumn years of her life. Nevertheless, Aunt Ange died four years after her biography appeared in the *Alumni Quarterly*. According to legend, she collapsed while organizing a section of biology books.[3] She was buried in Bloomington's Evergreen Cemetery, but for whatever reason did not have a headstone until a short time ago. Perhaps it was because the library was thought to be her eternal resting place, not the cold earth, or perhaps her original headstone was lost or stolen. Toni Tucker, a dean at Milner Library, speculated that Miss Milner did not have a headstone because she was a bachelorette who outlived all of her close relatives,[4] but it's difficult for me to believe that the university, her friends, or her colleagues would leave her without a memorial. One final possibility is that, in her humble manner, Ange specifically requested that a headstone not mark her grave.

In April 2006, one day after what would have been Miss Milner's 150th birthday, former Governor Rod Blagojevich, along with Mayor Chris Koos of Normal, Illinois, issued dual proclamations declaring April 10 "Angie Milner Day." Earlier that year, a team of librarians from Milner Library located what they believed to be Miss Milner's final resting place in Greenwood Cemetery. They raised money with the help of the University Foundation and purchased a headstone. "When we found out about her grave we felt that would be the best way to honor her legacy," Toni Tucker told the *Daily Vidette*. ISU Faculty and local politicians staged an unveiling ceremony for the monument on April 10.[5]

Since her death, Miss Milner's books have had no less than four homes. During the first half of her thirty-seven years as librarian of Normal University, Ange occupied a corner of the Old Main Building, which was damaged in a storm that struck the campus in 1902. The entire structure was torn down in 1959. In 1917, the university moved its library to North Hall, a Victorian Romanesque building designed by a local architect and built in 1892. Miss Milner worked there until she died. North Hall served as the library until 1940, when a new building was constructed and christened "Milner Library" to honor Normal University's beloved Aunt Ange. It was a fine example of neo-Georgian architecture designed by C. Herrick Hammond. In 1976, the old Milner Library became known as Williams Hall and most of the university's 675,000 books were moved into the new Milner Library, a square, concrete structure located on the north side of campus.[6] Many of the older books, still with call numbers hand written on the binding by Ange Milner herself, remained on the third floor of Williams Hall, which was used as the university archive.

Williams Hall

If Ange Milner never set foot in the library that originally bore her name, why is her ghost thought to haunt Williams Hall? For one thing, the two buildings in which she worked so diligently from 1890 to 1928 no longer exist. As previously mentioned, Old Main was torn down in 1959, and North Hall was demolished in 1965 to make room for more modern buildings. Troy Taylor, who has written extensively on the ghostlore of central Illinois, believed Ange haunts the books, not the building.[7] Since at least the 1980s, staff working in the archives have reported encounters with what they believe is the ghost of Ange Milner, still tending to her books.

It is unclear exactly when the stories of Ange Milner's ghost began to filter down from the third floor of Williams Hall. The earliest article I found in the *Daily Vidette* regarding the haunting appeared in October 1998, but Library Dean Cheryl Elzy told the *Pantagraph* that she had heard about the ghost going back to 1981.[8] Archive employees have reported eerie feelings, sightings of mist or fog, and even discovered books that inexplicably fell from the shelves. Their reflexive conclusion was that Ange Milner, or at least a part of her, had returned from the grave. Joan Winters, a former operations assistant at Milner Library, told Chandra Harris of the *Daily Vidette*, "The only thing that can explain her presence is her love for her books." Winter also related how, during an attempt to move some of the books, they "began tumbling to the floor by themselves." Another employee, Michael Lovell, said that he saw something "well-defined and white out of the corner of his eye."[9]

On Halloween night in 1998, a documentary by Jeff Felton called "Beyond Boundaries" aired on a local television station, TCI Channel 10. The 30-minute documentary covered Williams Hall, as well as an abandoned speakeasy in Decatur.[10] Felton's camera repeatedly malfunctioned while filming in the archive. "When they switched cameras, the new one wouldn't work either," the *Pantagraph* reported several years later, and Joan Winters added that the camera operator was so startled by the unexplainable malfunction that he refused to return to the archive.[11] In 2004, the Travel Channel included Williams Hall in its show "Haunted Campuses." Two ISU students, Sarah Smith and Shawn Joy, accompanied by a medium and film crew, investigated the haunting for the cable network. It turned out to be a very "spirited" evening. While the medium claimed to actually contact the ghost of Ange Milner, Miss Smith caught a glimpse of a white light, "rounded in front and flowing in the back, moving from one shelf on the left to another on the right." Shawn allegedly heard footsteps.[12]

Long after her retirement from the library, Joan Winters continued to relate to an eager audience various experiences with the ghost in Williams Hall. In 2004, she told the *Daily Vidette* that she had seen a full-torso apparition of the former librarian while working in the archive in 1995. She described it as "a five-foot tall elderly woman in a floor-length dress wearing her hair in a bun." A psychotherapist named Merlin Mather and his wife, Joan, also claimed to see a similar specter. "I went over to where she was, and what I saw was a kind of purple column of light," he related to the college newspaper. "Her skirt started to form. We could see the outline of it."[13] More than a few writers have commented on the similarities between these experiences and the opening scene of the movie *Ghostbusters* (1984), in which the main characters encountered the ghost of a librarian bathed in purple light, wearing a long skirt with her hair tied in a bun.

One possible explanation for the haunting in Williams Hall is the presence of infrasound. Infrasound describes a sound wave that travels at a speed below 15-20 cycles per minute, which is outside our range of hearing. These waves are frequently caused by earthquakes and other natural phenomenon, but can be generated by machines. The presence of infrasound waves have been known to produce paranoia, "creepy feelings," and even hallucinations in humans, which are caused when the sound waves vibrate the pupils of our eyes. According to Vic Tandy of Coventry University, the presence of an extractor fan in a reputedly haunted laboratory in Warwick caused him and others to experience feelings of dread, coldness, and even see formless shapes out of the corners of their eyes. When he turned the fan off, the strange experiences stopped. The fan was producing infrasound, which no one could hear and which was causing the laboratory employees to believe they were in the presence of something paranormal.[14]

Pantagraph reporter Roger Miller described the third floor of Williams Hall as claustrophobic, with "cool, musty air," and said that "the ventilation system rumbles in the background."[15] Perhaps this ventilation system produced more than just background noise? If it also generated infrasound waves, it would explain the feelings of not being alone, the cold spots, and the presence of "someone looking over your shoulder." It might also explain the spectral clouds and colors seen by some eyewitnesses, and the vibration caused by infrasound could explain why books fell off the shelves. Vic Tandy described eerily similar phenomena in his Warwick laboratory.

The new inhabitants of Williams Hall are in a unique position to test this theory, since both the University Archive and the old book collection were moved to other locations in the fall and winter of 2006. According to Jim Caselton, Distribution Clerk at Milner Library, some of the books were returned to the main library, and others were moved to a storage facility specially designed to maintain antique books. "They are housed in a much better environment than could be maintained

Williams Hall at
Illinois State University.

in Williams Hall," he recently informed me.[16] Has Ange Milner's ghost followed her books to their new location, or has she finally found peace? Only time will tell.

Watterson Towers

One more ghost is rumored to haunt Illinois State University, that of the architect who designed Watterson Towers, the tallest dormitory in the United States. An urban legend circulating the campus states that the architect (some mistakenly call him by the name Watterson, others claim he was the creator of Dungeons & Dragons, Gary Gygax) went insane and committed suicide. In reality, an architecture firm named Fridstein & Fitch of Chicago designed the towers, which opened in 1968, and they were named after Arthur W. Watterson, a professor of geography at ISU from 1946-1966. Professor Watterson *did not* commit suicide, but try telling that to students who swear the rumor is true. "Watterson was so upset over how the building turned out that he threw himself from the top," Brett Gould explained in his recent critical retelling of the legend in the *Daily Vidette*. Another rumor states, incredibly, that the architect designed the top floors of the building so they would fly off in the event of a tornado, and that the building sinks as much as an inch each year.[17]

The sinking building is a popular campus myth repeated at many universities around the country. Folklorist Jan Harold Brunvand has collected several accounts of such buildings, including one at Northwestern University in Chicago. There the library is rumored to have been built on land that was formerly part of Lake Michigan. As a result, the story goes, the building sinks a half an inch per year. The engineering building at the University of Pittsburgh is said to be gradually sliding down the hill on which it was built. None of these rumors are true, of course.[18]

Whether it is the ghost of Ange Milner, or the strange rumors surrounding Watterson Towers, Illinois State University has more than its fair share of folklore. The students and faculty of ISU have every reason to be proud of their university's rich history, interesting architecture, and the librarian who refuses to abandon the books and people she so dearly loved.

Chapter Endnotes

[1] Charles William Perry, "Angeline Vernon Milner," *The Alumni Quarterly* 13 (May 1924): 3.

[2] *Ibid.*, 7.

[3] *Daily Vidette* (Normal) 27 October 2004.

[4] *Daily Vidette* (Normal) 3 March 2006.

[5] *Daily Vidette* (Normal) 12 April 2006.

[6] *Daily Vidette* (Normal) 21 October 1975; "Historic Illinois States," *The Master Plan*, < http://www.masterplan.ilstu.edu/historic/> (10 May 2009).

[7] Troy Taylor, *Haunted Decatur Revisited: Ghostly Tales from the Haunted Heartland of Illinois* (Alton: Whitechapel Productions Press, 2000), 82.

[8] *Pantagraph* (Bloomington) 30 October 2000.

[9] *Daily Vidette* (Normal) 27 October 1998.

[10] *Daily Vidette* (Normal) 30 October 1998.

[11] *Pantagraph* (Bloomington) 30 October 2000.

[12] *Pantagraph* (Bloomington) 22 October 2004.

[13] *Daily Vidette* (Normal) 27 October 2004.

[14] William R. Corliss, *Handbook of Unusual Natural Phenomena: Eyewitness Accounts of Nature's Greatest Mysteries* (New York: Arlington House, 1986), 398-399; *Guardian* (London) 11 July 2000.

[15] *Pantagraph* (Bloomington) 30 October 2000.

[16] Jim Caselton, "RE: Question regarding the old books in Williams Hall," personal email (11 May 2009).

[17] *Daily Vidette* (Normal) 31 October 1997; *Daily Vidette* (Normal) 25 October 2002; *Daily Vidette* (Normal) 6 February 2009.

[18] Jan Harold Brunvand, *Too Good to Be True: The Colossal Book of Urban Legends* (New York: W. W. Norton & Company, 1999, 2001), 435.

Eastern Illinois University and the Legend of Pemberton Hall

Eastern Illinois University is a small university with a student population of around 11-12,000, located in the east-central Illinois town of Charleston. EIU was first established as a teacher's college in 1895, but didn't officially open until four years later. The university was then called Eastern Illinois State Normal School. Its mascot is a black panther, and anyone searching for southern Illinois' fabled panthers may find a statue of one a few feet from campus outside of Marty's bar, which has served the campus since 1973.

For such a small institution nestled in a quaint Midwestern town, EIU has produced its fair share of contributions to the cultural fabric of Illinois. Charleston was the birthplace of Jimmy John's, for instance, which had its first sandwich shop located in an alley across the street from ivy-covered Pemberton Hall, one of the campus dormitories.

Pemberton Hall is itself home to one of the most famous ghost stories in Illinois—the legend of Mary Hawkins—whose ghost is said to roam the hundred year old building, protecting the young women who reside within. Accounts of encounters with the ghost of Mary, interwoven with a popular urban legend, greet many a college bound girl as she finds herself away from home for the first time.

It is a story you may recognize.

It begins simply enough: Angela is staying in an all-girls dormitory at a public university that has just let out for break. For some reason, she is unable to go home like the other students. She shares the dorm with only two other individuals: a stern headmistress named Mary and a lonely and eccentric janitor.

With nothing else to pass the time, Angela leaves her room and ascends to a quiet corner of the fourth floor to play the piano. As she settles onto the bench and begins to play, she is unaware that the janitor has crept up behind her. Leaving her no time to scream, he attacks—perpetrating unspeakable acts upon her body with a knife or an axe before running off to parts unknown.

With her last ounce of strength, Angela drags herself to the headmistress' room for help. Mary, however, has locked the door and gone to sleep. She is unable to hear the student's scratches and garbled pleas. The next morning, Mary opens her door to find Angela dead in the hallway with her fingernails embedded in the wood. Stricken with grief, Mary loses her mind and spends the rest of her tortured life in a state hospital.

This is one variation of a story known to folklorists as "The Roommate's Death." First written down by Linda Dégh in her essay "The Roommate's Death and Related Dormitory Stories in Formation" in *Indiana Folklore* 2 (1969), she had heard it from a student at Indiana University who had been told the story as a freshman in 1964. In the original version, the killing took place in a sorority house, and it was the victim's roommates who discovered her body. Todd Webb, in *Too Good to Be True* by Jan Harold Brunvand, wrote that he first heard the story while he was an undergrad in Georgia in 1983. The incident, interestingly, was alleged to have occurred at the University of Illinois in Champaign-Urbana. The story is told, Brunvand explained, "as a warning to freshmen by upperclass students or by resident advisors in the dormitories."[1] It is a story that feeds on the fears of college-bound women all over the country.

Thanks to unabating interest, the version of "The Roommate's Death" told at Eastern Illinois University has taken on a life of its own. The victim and the victim's unfortunate guardian have both transcended their ordeal and now haunt the hall as ghosts. Over the years, an old plaque dedicated to one of the first directors of Pemberton Hall, a popular urban legend, and a touch of wishful thinking have combined to create one of the most enduring oral traditions in east-central Illinois. The story itself is incredible, but in this case, the truth behind it is almost stranger than fiction.

Pemberton Hall is the oldest all-female dormitory in the state of Illinois and was the brainchild of Livingston C. Lord, president of Eastern Illinois State Normal School from 1899 to 1933. In 1901, President Lord went before the Appropriations Committee of the Illinois state legislature and asked for $60,000 to build a woman's dormitory on campus. The committee denied the funding after telling the staunchly nonpartisan Lord that he "had made a fairly good joke."[2] One senator, Stanton C. Pemberton, took the idea seriously and began to lobby on President Lord's behalf.

Finally, in 1907, President Lord and Senator Pemberton plied $100,000 out of the legislature for both a dorm and an accompanying gymnasium. Two years later, as the construction neared its final stages, the state Appropriations Committee added $3,000 to finish the basement and the attic. The completed hall, named after Senator Pemberton, housed up to 100 women and officially opened on January 4, 1909. Miss Estelle Gross became the first headmistress, but only served in the position for a year before being succeeded by the now infamous Mary E. Hawkins.[3] Senator Pemberton was enamored with the new dorm, which he said possessed "a fine high-sounding name." President Lord was also proud of the building and once remarked, "I never go by in the evening when the

Pemberton Hall at Eastern Illinois University.
Photo by the author.

girls are in their rooms and the lights [are on] in all the windows without feeling anew the satisfaction of it."[4]

The old-English look and feel of the dormitory was well suited for its first full-time matron, Mary Hawkins, who emigrated from Great Britain in 1901 and possessed all the stoic air of an Edwardian Englishwoman. Recent accounts of Mary as being in her twenties and possessing long, blonde hair are wholly inaccurate. In reality, she was a pleasant looking woman with curly, dark hair that she pinned up in the fashion of her day.[5] Born in 1877, Miss Hawkins assumed the position of dorm director in August 1910 when she was thirty-three years old. "As head of Pemberton Hall," she once wrote, "[the residents] are under my control entirely."[6] She had no patience for libertine college life and imposed strict rules on "her girls," which included a 7:30pm curfew and 10:30pm bedtime. Church was the only place coeds were able to go unchaperoned.

Mary Hawkins left her position at Pemberton Hall in March 1917 and died at the age of forty-one on the night of October 29, 1918 at the Kankakee State Mental Hospital in the shadow of the influenza epidemic and the end of the First World War. Hospital orderlies discovered her body at 5am the next day. Her obituary read: "she was a woman of education and refinement and a most efficient person in the position she occupied. Very seldom, indeed, does one find in the same individual good business ability, a most excellent housekeeper, and a fine influence over young women."[7] Her death certificate listed the cause of death as "general paralysis of the insane," otherwise known as general paresis, a condition of motor paralysis and softening of the brain.[8] General paresis occurs as a result of late-term, or tertiary, syphilis, which sets in a decade or more after infection and triggers abnormal eye reflexes, dementia, dramatic mood swings, and even seizures. Two years after Mary's death, the university hung a bronze tablet near the entrance commemorating her service. The tablet remains there to this day.

It is unclear exactly when urban legend and historical fact merged to create the unique tale of the ghost of Mary Hawkins. Storytellers cannot even agree on which character the name of Mary belongs to—the murdered coed or the distraught dorm mother. Sometimes Mary manifests herself as a prankster; a young woman who scratches at doors, leaves footprints, or wanders up to the fourth floor dressed in nothing but a white gown. Other times Mary is a benevolent matriarch who makes sure doors are locked at night and warns her girls of trouble. Some writers have attempted to clear up the confusion by suggesting that two ghosts may be at work; one of the unfortunate victim and the other of Mary Hawkins, who has come back from the dead to watch over her girls as she once did in life.[9]

The earliest article I found concerning the Pemberton Hall legend was written by Karen Knupp in October 1976 for the *Eastern News*. Karen explained that the story, having been told for "years and years," was handed down from veteran Pem Hall residents to incoming freshmen through an oral tradition that included using the story as a topic in their speech classes. Numbered among the eerie proceedings she chronicled were a girl who saw a light emanating from one of the windows on the fourth floor, a resident assistant who found that the lounge furniture rearranged itself, and a strange encounter with a girl wearing a white gown who went around asking for safety pins before she disappeared. Karen noted that some residents had celebrated their unique heritage by holding a "Mary Hawkins Day" the previous spring.[10]

In November of the same year, Karen wrote a follow-up article after a 1921 resident of Pemberton Hall named Stella (Craft) Temple contacted her and told her that she knew the origins of the ghost story. Mrs. Temple explained that a coed named Uterpa Sharps, a thirty-year-old student with an interest in hypnotism, liked to scare the younger girls by jumping out of the janitor's closet. Mrs. Temple, who if she had actually lived there in 1921 could not have known Mary Hawkins (who would have been deceased at that time), claimed that, "no one would tell Miss Hawkins. She wouldn't have any monkey business like that. She was English and very strict." If it was true she knew Mary Hawkins, then the events featuring Uterpa Sharps must have taken place before 1917. At any rate, she suggested that Uterpa's strange behavior was the origin of the legend, not a murder.[11]

After some investigation, I discovered that Euterpe Sharp (as her name was actually spelled) graduated from Eastern in 1919. Euterpe served as illustrator for the 1919 Eastern yearbook, the *Warbler*, and also participated in making crafts for a visiting third grade class in December. Her senior quote was "it is better to wear out than to rust out."[12] Oddly enough, I found no mention of Estella (as her name was actually spelled) Craft in 1919, 1920, or 1921. She was, however, listed among the senior class in 1922.[13] That means, if these events are to be believed, that Estella must have been a freshman when Euterpe was a senior. Regardless, she could not have gone to Eastern when Mary Hawkins served as dorm mother, and it is likely that her recollections of Mary were passed down to her from other residents.

Because Mary departed Eastern during the First World War, most storytellers allege the murder occurred around that time. Some have used the sporadic publication of the school's newspaper, which was actually the result of war rationing, as proof of a conspiracy to cover up the crime. The details of when either Mary or the coed met their unfortunate end have changed periodically. There exists a general consensus that the murder took place over winter break, but an October 1984 *Daily Eastern News* article written by Diane Schneidman suggested May as the month it occurred, and an article published in 1982 claimed it transpired during Spring Break.[14] Jo-Anne Christensen, in her book *Ghost Stories of Illinois*, depicted the crime being committed during a furious thunderstorm, which also suggests springtime. The *National Directory of Haunted Places*, written by Dennis William Hauck, challenged all of those accounts by changing the year of the murder to 1920, long after the real Mary Hawkins was deceased.[15]

The details of the incident, including why and how Mary or the girl were killed, where they stayed in Pemberton, and even who killed them, have also changed over the years, and the accounts have become quite inventive. Diane Schneidman, for example, wrote that the homicidal janitor's wife had died, implying that grief and desperation drove him to murder. Some writers, such as *Daily Eastern News* staff writer Jennifer Lavery, have weaved other historical events into the narrative. Not realizing that Mary Hawkins had no relatives living in the United States, Jennifer believed that a John Hawkins, who appeared in the Coles County court records in May 1917, had gone to trial for the murder of his "sister" Mary. "I think I finally found some truth to this supposed rumor," she wrote.[16]

During one of the notorious haunted houses held in Pemberton Hall, the guide told visitors that Mary's room had been number 308. One student attending that particular event told the *Daily Eastern News* reporters that Mary had been having an affair with a married professor before she was killed.[17] The murder weapon, though usually consistent, has changed as well. With a variety any fan of the game Clue would appreciate, it has been alternatively described as an axe, a blunt object, bare hands, and even piano wire.

In 1984, William M. Michael, a writer for the Decatur *Herald and Review*, spent the night in the fourth floor piano room. Needless to say, he reported no encounters with a ghost. But for every tale of disappointment, there is one that seems to confirm that something strange is taking place inside the ninety-nine year old walls. The same day that Michael's article was printed, a story appeared alongside it that recounted one woman's experience with the ghost. Patty O'Neill, also a writer for the *Herald and Review*, lived in Pemberton Hall for three years and claimed that she had awoken one night in the spring of 1981 to see a young woman dressed in a nightgown standing beside her bed. Thinking it was her roommate, she tried to ask the girl what was wrong, but the intruder turned around and walked away without a reply.[18] Patty's eerie tale was reprinted in Beth Scott and Michael Norman's book *Haunted America*, which launched the story of Mary Hawkin's ghost to national fame.

Another bizarre incident occurred in 1984 when one Pemberton Hall resident discovered small, black footprints that appeared on the floor of her room. "They seemed to be the prints of someone tip-toeing across the room, and the prints proved impossible to remove," assistant editor Michelle Mueller wrote in the *Verge* section of the *Daily Eastern News*. "The prints led from the door to the closet and back out to the door."[19] Other experiences included doors locking and unlocking, furniture moving by itself, electronic disturbances, and the faint sounds of footsteps or a piano playing on the fourth floor. One former resident director even claimed that her fiancé felt someone smack him on the rear end even though she was on the other side of the room.[20]

Kelly Bryan, a Pem Hall resident in 2002 and 2004, told me that she never experienced anything unusual while living there and didn't believe in the story, although she noted that the basement always gave her the creeps. "From what I've read, I just don't think it has much basis in reality," she said. "If you really believe in it, you're more likely to blame things on the ghost."[21]

Over the years, Pemberton Hall has opened its doors, as well as its notorious fourth floor, around Halloween in an effort to raise money and entertain students with the story. According to an article by Bob Glover in the *Daily Eastern News*, the tradition of turning Pem Hall into a haunted house began in 1978. "The stories that have haunted Pemberton Hall and the secrets of the fourth floor will finally be available for public scrutiny," Glover wrote. "On Saturday, the one and only fourth floor will be opened for the first time in many, many years."[22] The event was repeated the next year for a small fifty-cent fee. Apparently the experience wasn't well received, since the Resident Housing Association haunted house was moved to an abandoned residence on Seventh Street in 1983. "The act will be more convincing than the usual RHA haunted house at Pemberton Hall," the project chairman commented in an article about the move.[23] The haunted house did add its own contribution to the legend, however, when drops of fake blood were left on the floor and the piano keys, giving a chill to anyone who was lucky enough to venture up there. Pemberton Hall resumed its haunted house in 1997, complete with an actress playing the X-Files theme on the fourth floor piano and a man in a black robe who told the story to the groups of bemused college students.[24] The Pemberton Hall Council opened the dorm once again in 2001, although the haunted house was strictly confined to its lower levels. Because of safety concerns, visitors were only allowed to "peek" at the mysterious fourth floor.[25]

Social commentary has crept its way into the telling of the Mary Hawkins story, most often in the form of brief snipes at Mary's "strict rules." Margaret Allen-Kline, in her Master's thesis on the tale, went one step farther, speculating that "there are warnings within these stories, warnings regarding consequences for women who go against established gender roles, women who allow themselves to remain unprotected, isolated from society or community."[26] Jan Harold Brunvand agreed, citing conclusions by folklorist Beverly Crane in his analysis of "The Roommate's Death" that the story contains a lesson in woman's liberation.[27]

Therefore the story of Mary Hawkins has, occasionally, fitted neatly into a narrative wherein her ghostly manifestations are the result of a battle between the (allegedly) draconian rules of the turn of the century and the libertine college life of our contemporary era. The idea that Mary's stringent rules were an engine of gender oppression, however, is as much a part of the myth as the ghost stories themselves. While conservative by today's standards, the college and university of Mary Hawkins' time was a progressive institution in which mainstream Protestant values coexisted with modern scientific methods. The entire campus, not just the women's dorm, was administrated like a military camp. Along with its basic courses, education was designed to teach students conformity to rules, self-discipline, and self-restraint; values that, as Mary's own unfortunate death illustrates, were sometimes difficult to live up to.

It is easy for someone living today to paint the period with a wide brush, but not everyone at the time had the same opinion in regards to gender relations. Livingston C. Lord, for instance, had no patience for conservative attacks on co-ed activities, and in 1909, when a student at Eastern joined a local preacher in condemning the dances held on campus, President Lord thought of him as a "hypocrite" and a "sneak and a liar" who "was talking filth about the girls." Some of the young man's fellow students even tossed him into the campus pond. During the course of another series of evangelical revivals in the community, President Lord took a female student aside and told her, "Don't let anyone tell you, you are bad or wicked—because you are not."[28]

As Pemberton Hall passes its 100-year anniversary, interest in the legend of Mary Hawkins seems unabated. Its inclusion in books on Illinois ghost stories has become obligatory, and a steady rotation of students arriving each year at Eastern Illinois University guarantees that the story will be passed down from one generation to the next. For the young women of Pemberton Hall, the spirit of Mary Hawkins will always be there with them; watching, protecting, and playing pranks.

Chapter Endnotes

[1] Jan Harold Brunvand, *Too Good to Be True: The Colossal Book of Urban Legends* (New York: W. W. Norton & Company, 1999, 2001), 433-434.

[2] *Eastern News* (Charleston) 22 October 1965.

[3] Ibid.

[4] Charles H. Coleman, *Eastern Illinois State College: Fifty Years of Public Service* in *Eastern Illinois State College Bulletin* 189 (January 1950): 123; Isabel McKinney, *Mr. Lord: The Life and Words of Livingston C. Lord* (Urbana: University of Illinois Press, 1937), 237-238.

[5] Troy Taylor's description of her as having long blond hair is inaccurate, not to mention anachronistic. See: *The '13 Wapper* (Charleston: Eastern Illinois State Normal School, 1913), 16.

[6] *Eastern News* (Charleston) 19 April 1967.

[7] *Daily Courier* (Charleston) 31 October 1918.

[8] Margaret Allen-Kline, "'She Protects Her Girls': The Legend of Mary Hawkins at Pemberton Hall" (M.A. thesis, Eastern Illinois University, 1998), 6.

[9] *Eastern News* (Charleston) 25 October 1979.

[10] *Eastern News* (Charleston) 15 October 1976.

[11] *Eastern News* (Charleston) 5 November 1976.

[12] *The Warbler*, vol. 1, (Charleston: Eastern Illinois State Normal School, 1919), 8-9, 32, 64.

[13] *The Warbler*, vol. 4, (Charleston: Eastern Illinois State Normal School, 1922), 29.

[14] *Daily Eastern News* (Charleston) 26 October 1984; *Daily Eastern News* (Charleston) 29 October 1982.

[15] Jo-Anne Christensen, *Ghost Stories of Illinois* (Edmonton: Lone Pine Publishing, 2000), 189; Dennis William Hauck, *Haunted Places: The National Directory: Ghostly Abodes, Sacred Sites, UFO Landings, and Other Supernatural Locations* (New York: Penguin Books, 1994, 1996), 153.

[16] *Daily Eastern News* (Charleston) 2 November 1989.

[17] *Daily Eastern News* (Charleston) 31 October 1997.

[18] *Herald and Review* (Decatur) 25 October 1984; see also: Allen-Kline, 54.

[19] *Daily Eastern News* (Charleston) 25 October 1985.

[20] Allen-Kline, 74.

[21] Kelly Bryan, interview by author, September 2006.

[22] *Daily Eastern News* (Charleston) 27 October 1978.

[23] *Daily Eastern News* (Charleston) 28 October 1983.

[24] *Daily Eastern News* (Charleston) 31 October 1997.

[25] *Daily Eastern News* (Charleston) 31 October 2001.

[26] Allen-Kline, 34.

[27] Jan Harold Brunvand, *The Vanishing Hitchhiker: American Urban Legends and Their Meanings* (New York: W.W. Norton & Company, 1981), 61.

[28] McKinney, 238-240.

Part 3
Rivers and Roads

The Cambridge "Death Curve"

Life is slow in Henry County, Illinois. With 86.7 percent of its land devoted to agriculture, the most commotion a visitor is likely to hear comes from tractors rumbling across the land as farmers plow their fields. Cambridge, the county seat, is a village of little more than 2,000 residents. Less than a mile outside of Cambridge sits Timber Ridge Road. As motorists travel west along Timber Ridge, they encounter a sharp curve marked by a Mulberry tree and an old, rustic fence that divides two cornfields. Here the wind gently caresses the grass along the roadside, but this bucolic scene hides a dark history, a history that few would remember if it weren't for the ghost stories whispered from one generation to another. The stories concern a crime eerily similar to one we are familiar with today, only the murders committed near this curve were much more brutal, if equally horrifying.

In June 2001, many Americans were shocked by the story of Andrea Yates, a deeply religious mother who drowned her five children. Years before the murders, Yates and her husband had fallen under the spell of a preacher named Michael Woroniecki. Woroniecki, in addition to encouraging them to have as many children as possible, frequently berated Andrea and her husband for their ungodly behavior. Andrea already had four children when she suffered a mental breakdown and attempted suicide in 1999. Her psychiatrist counseled her not to have any more children, but in 2000 Andrea and her husband conceived a fifth child even after she had been hospitalized for her condition. During the spring of 2001, her mental health rapidly deteriorated until, one tragic day in June, she drowned all five children in their bathtub. She placed the bodies of the four youngest on the bed next to each other and covered them with a sheet. Later, while in jail, Andrea told a psychiatrist, "My children weren't righteous... The way I was raising them, they could never be saved. They were doomed to perish in the fires of hell."[1]

The Yates case raised awareness of postpartum depression, a mental illness which affects a very small percentage of mothers who have just given birth. While this alone does not explain why a woman would commit filicide, a history of depression is one of the highest risk factors for postpartum depression.[2] The illness was unknown in 1905 when one deeply emotionally disturbed woman in rural Illinois, Julia Markham, used an ax to take the lives of her seven children. Like Andrea Yates, Julia had previous episodes of severe depression and a history of attempted suicide. Other elements of the two incidents were uncomfortably similar, but one stark contrast was that in 1905, although the story of the Markham murders found its way into several local newspapers, the national media never picked up on the tragedy. There were no interviews or book deals. Julia's heinous crime faded from memory and became nothing more than legend.

The murders, however, were all too real. In 1896, Julia Johnson married a man from Andover named Clarence B. Markham, and the young couple settled down on a farm in Andover Township outside of Cambridge, Illinois. Although Julia had a colored past, by all accounts the Markhams began a happy and prosperous life together. Ten years before their marriage, when Julia was 13 years old, she tried to commit suicide by jumping in a well, but was rescued. Her mother, Mary E. Johnson, had a history of mental illness. According to the *Cambridge Chronicle*, she had been "mentally deranged for some time," and at the time of the murders she was in the insane annex at the county hospital in Knoxville. She was committed there on September 13 for "wandering spells."[3]

In nine years of marriage, Mrs. Markham gave birth to seven children, an average of one every fifteen months. There were four girls and three boys, aged from between five months to eight and a half years. Their names were Clara, Harry, Charles, Mary, Lucy, Eliza, and Asa. Coincidentally, Andrea Yates' youngest child was six months old at the time of the drowning, but Andrea had drawn a bath a month earlier with the same sinister intention.[4] Something happened during the first five months after the birth of both Julia and Andrea's youngest that led them to contemplate murder. Whether it was the stress of feeding so many mouths, or depression triggered by the births, we will never know. Julia Markham died along with her children, leaving behind only a short letter to give a glimpse of her motivation.

On the morning of Saturday September 30, 1905, while her husband labored in a neighboring field, Julia Markham, to quote the *Cambridge Chronicle*, "committed one of the most dastardly deeds that has ever occurred in Henry County." At around eleven o'clock, Julia sent her two eldest children to a nearby spring to retrieve water. While they were gone, she took an ax and swung it at the heads of her five youngest, killing them instantly. When her eldest returned, she dealt with them the same way. One can only imagine the horror of the scene inside that house. Julia had carefully planned the massacre and intended to commit suicide afterward, but the knife that she used to cut her throat was too dull. Reeling from the wound, she laid her children out on a

The Cambridge
Death Curve.

bed, side by side, and doused them with coal oil. She lit the oil on fire and the entire house went up in flames. She intended to die with her children, but the heat of the conflagration proved to be too much and she tried to crawl to safety.

Meanwhile, the Markham's neighbors saw smoke billowing from the house and rushed over. Intending to save the children, they instead stumbled upon a terrible scene. "Mrs. Markham stayed in the burning house until practically all her clothing was burned off, and then crawled out doors," the *Chronicle* reported. Sheriff B.H. Stiers and his deputy, a Mr. E.A. Swain, along with a doctor from Woodhull, quickly arrived and found Julia clutching to life. Dr. Clanahan stitched the wound in Julia's throat, but informed her that she didn't have long to live. Seeing the end was finally near, she confessed to the crime and died at three o'clock that afternoon. "The sufferings of the woman from the self inflicted knife wounds and severe burns were something dreadful," wrote the *Chronicle*. However, "she seemed perfectly sane after the deed had been committed."[5]

Despite her appearance after the murders, a coroner's jury later ruled that Julia had acted while temporarily insane. An investigation into her personal history revealed that she had suffered from an emotional breakdown several months before the crime. "As early as July Mrs. Markham manifested symptoms of a diseased mind," the Rock Island *Argus* reported. Her father visited the family during the summer and said that Julia was suffering from "extreme melancholia, due... to the dreary monotony and drudgery of her life." Her eldest children had to stay home from school to watch after her health.[6]

The house was completely consumed by flames, and the sheriff found the bodies of the children in a corner of the smoldering ruins. They were burned beyond recognition. Shortly thereafter, a postman discovered a letter Julia had written to her husband, proving the murders had been premeditated. "Dear Clarence," she wrote. "This is to say goodbye to you. Some give their souls for others, and I will do this for my children. God bless them! They will all die happy in the arms of Jesus. I will meet them there, and some day you will join us, too." On the morning of October 2, as the Wright brothers prepared for the flight of their third airplane, Julia Markham and her children were laid to rest in nearby Rose Dale Cemetery. The children were interred in one casket and Julia in another. Distraught over the gruesome deaths of his wife and children, Clarence Markham moved away from the area.

Decades passed, and the ruin of the Markham's home was plowed over. Their aging, red barn remained, however, and became a focal point for local teens who grew up hearing stories about the murders. Fact blended with fiction, and people began to report seeing the ghost of Julia Markham along the roadside. They blamed accidents at the curve in Timber Ridge Road on her ghost.

The particulars of the case became ever more confused. Like a generational game of phone tag, each retelling of the tale altered the details until the fact that a woman murdered her children became the only kernel of truth. For instance, the story according to an anonymous contributor to Strangeusa.com was that Clarence Markham died of an illness, leaving his wife to take care of their seven children. "So one day she took her kids lined them up in a line in the front yard. And she decapitated each one," the post read. "When she realized what she had done she set her house on fire and shot herself in the head." From then on, at exactly 10:27pm Julia's ghost could be seen sitting on the fencepost near what became known as "Death Curve."[7]

In 2007, the Moline *Dispatch* ran an article on the Cambridge Death Curve that featured one eyewitness account of the haunting from eighteen years earlier. The red barn was still standing at the time, and two young women drove out there looking for a place to hang out. As they neared the curve, they caught sight of something unexpected. "On the fence, you could see something white floating off into the cornfield," one of the women told the newspaper. "It was white with long flowing hair... I didn't know what the heck it was."[8] But a translucent phantom was not the only thing spotted along the road. Paranormal researchers Chad Lewis and Terry Fisk spoke with one woman who told them that she had seen a spook light floating near the old fence.[9]

There is nothing unusual about the curve in Timber Ridge Road, even less so now that the dilapidated barn has been torn down. The graves of Julia Markham and her children are unmarked. Aside from a few articles on dusty microfilm reels, nothing tangible remains that would remind passersby of the unspeakable acts committed outside the village of Cambridge that fateful day in 1905. Yet the act of a mother murdering her own children—something so anathema to our basic values—is a stain that will not be so easily removed. Even after a hundred years, the spirits of Julia and her children cry out from the grave, never to be forgotten.

Chapter Endnotes

[1]*Houston Chronicle* (Houston) 6 March 2002.

[2]Sarah J. Breese McCoy, et al., "Risk Factors for Postpartum Depression: A Retrospective Investigation at 4-Weeks Postnatal and a Review of the Literature," *The Journal of the American Osteopathic Association* 106 (April 2006): 193-198.

[3]*Cambridge Chronicle* (Cambridge) 5 October 1905.

[4]Suzanne O'Malley, *Are You There Alone?: The Unspeakable Crime of Andrea Yates* (New York: Simon and Schuster, 2004), 20.

[5]*Cambridge Chronicle* (Cambridge) 5 October 1905.

[6]*The Argus* (Rock Island) 30 September 1905; *The Argus* (Rock Island) 2 October 1905.

[7]Anonymous, "Death Curve," 1 June 2005, <http://strangeusa.com/viewlocation.aspx?locationid=2850> (21 May 2009).

[8]*The Dispatch* (Moline) 19 May 2007.

[9]Chad Lewis and Terry Fisk, *The Illinois Road Guide to Haunted Locations* (Eau Claire: Unexplained Research Publishing Company, 2007), 135.

Airtight Bridge

On a typical autumn evening, as Charlie and his girlfriend Megan left the campus of Eastern Illinois University to enjoy a game of miniature golf at Lincoln Springs Resort, they found themselves driving down a rural route somewhere northeast of Charleston. As fate would have it, the sun had gone down before the two could find their way back to a main road, and Charlie hadn't bothered to bring a map. As trees and fields flew past, it was clear they were getting further and further away from their destination.

Tensions were already running high when their headlights fell on two pairs of eyes that shimmered near the mailbox of a white, double-wide trailer. As Charlie's silver Mitsubishi Outlander drove past, two unleashed dogs jumped at the vehicle and pursued it to the edge of the paved road, where they were lost in the dirt and dust kicked up by the Outlander as it ground the chalky gravel under its wheels. Navigating several sharp curves, Megan and Charlie's hearts raced as the road pitched downward and the fallow cornfields disappeared behind thick woods and desolate meadows. Charlie slowed down to avoid spinning out, and everything became eerily quiet aside from the sound of tires against the road.

Charlie threw his girlfriend a worried glance as they approached a small, white sign warning of a weight limit of eight tons. Suddenly the trestles of an old, one lane suspension bridge loomed out of the darkness. The branches of two large trees, a sycamore and a bur oak, formed a natural arch over the foreboding entrance. Lurching forward, the Outlander rolled over the broken pavement suspended fifteen and a half feet above the inky waters of the Embarras River. For a moment, the burgundy, steel supports were all the two saw in every direction.

As Charlie and Megan reached the opposite entrance, their headlights revealed an old greeting spray-painted onto the guardrail that cryptically read, "Howdy Grimster." The sounds of nature returned after the two had crossed the sixty-yard distance to the other side.

That night, Charlie and Megan had inadvertently stumbled upon Airtight Bridge, one of Coles County's best kept secrets. Located along Airtight Road, it is the only direct route between the village of Ashmore and the unincorporated towns of Bushton and Rardin. It is isolated and remote. Most people do not come upon it by accident. The bridge itself is interesting enough, but it was a gruesome discovery there over twenty-five years ago on the banks of the Embarras River that really ignited the local imagination. Since that time, visitors have returned from nightly excursions with many unusual tales to tell.

Locals say the bridge earned the name "Airtight" because of the unnatural stillness encountered while crossing it. If a visitor were to stand in the middle of the bridge, he or she might hear the rumble of some distant tractor, or the wind in the trees, but that would be all. Nancy Shick, a member of the Coles County Historical Society, told the *Daily Eastern News* that the name came about because air settles in the forested valley where the bridge is located.[1] While the origin of its name is uncertain, this much we know: the bridge was designed by Claude L. James and built in 1914 by the Decatur Bridge Company. Thanks to its remote location, it became known as a drinking spot for local teens and students from Eastern Illinois University. During the 1950s it was a hangout for the Black Knights of the Embarras, a club that ranged up and down east central Illinois, and in the late 1960s and '70s it was frequented by an Illinois chapter of the Sons of Silence, a "one-percenter" motorcycle gang. Otherwise, the bridge, which even thirty years ago was described as "old" and "creaky," had a pretty mundane existence. In 1981, it was added to the National Register of Historic Places on account of "event, Architecture/Engineering."[2]

That "event" was the discovery, one year prior, of the nude body of a woman floating near the bank of the Embarras River a few yards downstream from Airtight Bridge. Because the body was missing its head, hands, and feet, the murder investigation became known as the "Airtight torso case." It came at the painful end to an unrelated series of murders of young women in Coles County going back nearly a decade. The Airtight case, like the other murders, remains unsolved.

It was a pleasant Sunday morning on October 19, 1980. The trees were in full autumn colors and in two days Molly Hatchet was set to perform at nearby Eastern Illinois University. William and Tim Brown, two brothers from rural Urbana, were on a deer hunting trip when they took the road down to Airtight at around eleven o'clock. As they crossed the bridge, one of the brothers noticed something unusual in the shallow waters of the Embarras, so they pulled over to the side of the road. At the same time, a local farmer named Victor Hargis was on his way to assist his son in digging a well. Seeing both the men and the partially decomposed remains, he stopped and joined William in going down to the river's edge to take a closer look. The two could hardly believe their eyes.

Victor sprang into action. He drove home and called the Sheriff's Department. Darrell Cox, a deputy at the time, was at the firing range when he got the call. It took him nearly twenty minutes to navigate the back roads from Charleston to the bridge, but he was familiar with the route because it was one the Sheriff's Department routinely patrolled. Recalling his first impression of the crime scene, Mr. Cox, now the county sheriff, told the *Daily Eastern News*, "I could tell from when I got there that [the body] was missing its head and feet... I remember when I first saw it standing on the bridge, it didn't look like a person."[3]

As police cordoned off the bridge and word spread of the discovery, reporters and television crews descended on the remote location. The gruesome nature of the crime caused a sensation, and the story remained in the headlines for three days. Moreover, it was the second time in three years that a body had been found at a popular hangout along the Embarras River in rural Coles County. In 1977, a local man named Andy Lanman died of a massive drug overdose at a spot south of Charleston known as "The Cellar." He was missing for twenty-five days before hunters stumbled upon his morphine-saturated body near the river.[4]

Back at Airtight Bridge, police worked into the evening using scuba divers to scour the river for clues. But the missing body parts, which had been severed "fairly cleanly," were never found. The cause of death was also never determined. Coles County Coroner Dick Lynch described the woman as being in her twenties, "rather flat-chested," "not in the habit of shaving," about 5 feet 9 inches, weighing around 130 pounds, with dark auburn hair. He deduced that she had not been dead more than a day or so, and that she had been killed somewhere other than at the bridge. Coles County Sheriff Chuck Lister agreed. He believed the woman had been murdered and then dismembered, at which point the perpetrator(s) drove to Airtight with her body and "rolled [it] down the bridge embankment." Her remains were immediately shipped to Springfield to be examined by pathologist Dr. Grant Johnson at Memorial Medical Center, but he was unable to uncover anything conclusive because of the advanced state of decomposition and lack of vital extremities.[5]

In Dr. Johnson's initial examination, he determined that the woman had an uncommon "A-positive" blood type, which may have aided in the identification of her remains had any immediate family come forward to report a missing person. She did not have any major scars, birthmarks, or tattoos that might have given a clue as to her identity, nor was it easy to determine the time of death. "Observers seem to be fairly certain that the body was not on the riverbank early the preceding evening," Dr. Johnson concluded in his final report. "The lack of rigidity and the early decomposition changes would certainly suggest that the body had been dead longer than the preceding evening and had been brought from some other location to the bank of the river." He estimated that the victim had not been deceased for more than forty-eight hours at

Airtight Bridge, Coles Cou

the time of discovery. Aside from trace amounts of aspirin, there were no drugs, poisons, or alcohol in her bloodstream, and no evidence of rape or abuse. Without the head or hands, and without any abrasions on the body, it was impossible for the coroner to even determine if a struggle preceded death. Tragically, it did appear, however, that the victim may at one time have been pregnant.[6]

Investigators heralded the determination of the blood type as an important clue in a case that was rapidly going cold. Sheriff Lister told the Journal Gazette that it "could narrow things down significantly." Unfortunately, he also revealed that checks of missing persons reports "failed to produce any substantial leads." There were several missing persons called in around the time the body was discovered, but they all concerned much younger individuals. A sack of clothes was found north of Charleston, but investigators quickly concluded it had no relevance to the case.[7] By Thursday, October 23, the Sheriff's Department suspended the search for clues in and around the river.

Reporters examined the story from every conceivable angle, but as the evidence remained thin and no new leads were uncovered, it quietly faded from the headlines. Nearly a year after her discovery, the unidentified body was laid to rest in Charleston's Mound Cemetery under the name "Jane Doe." Those who remembered the case occasionally traveled to her grave and left flowers or other tokens of their sympathy.

The Airtight case lay dormant until the mid 1980s, when a convict named Henry Lee Lucas briefly confessed to the murder. Lucas, who died in prison in 2001, was either an unabashed liar or one of the most prolific serial killers in American history. Between 1975 and his arrest in 1983, Lucas and a man named Ottis Toole roamed the heartland, killing at least eleven victims before being apprehended in Texas. While in prison, Lucas confessed to a staggering 600 homicides. Investigators from around the country brought him their cold cases, and he expressed complicity in one after the other. The task force set up to investigate his claims was, in many instances, all too eager to accept them at face value.[8] Inevitably, Lucas confessed to the Airtight Bridge murder, and the Coles County Sheriff's Department excitedly announced the news.

Mark Temples was a reporter in Charleston at the time, and he was close to many of the detectives working on the case. "I had just done a seven part [radio] series on the Airtight murder, a more extensive series than anyone had ever done on it," he told me. "We were all enjoying the day off one day, and I got a phone call here from Chuck Lister, the sheriff, who wanted me to be at the courthouse for a press conference. I said, 'well, about what?' and he said, 'believe me, you'll want to be there.'"

Sheriff Lister announced that the perpetrator in the Airtight case had been found and that an indictment would be forthcoming. "The way he put it, it was going to be a formality, that it was a slam dunk," Mark Temples explained. Henry Lee Lucas, the man in question, had made a deal with ABC News to tell his story, an embellished tale filled with mayhem and murder, but then recanted when he felt the network had not held up its end of the bargain. "So everybody in the nation who had a murder on the books went to see this man," Mark said. "In the Airtight case, he told them he couldn't remember [the victim's] name, which was unusual, but he did remember Airtight Bridge and he did remember picking her up in east Texas, bringing her to... Missouri where he killed her and dismembered her, and he dumped off the body at Airtight, the hands at another location, and the head at another location." The Illinois State Police conducted an extensive search for the missing parts, but found nothing. "The grand jury blew up in Lister's face and they never returned an indictment," Mark added.

Still, there was compelling evidence to link Henry Lee Lucas to the crime. "He drew a map directly from Danville, Illinois to Airtight," Mr. Temples explained, "and I know locals who can't even do that... I don't think [Sheriff Lister] would have convened a press conference to that extent unless he thought he had it in the bag." At one point, Mark spoke directly over the phone to Lucas, who changed his story and adamantly denied any role in the Airtight murder.[9] "He was just confessing to anything and everything he could to keep talking," Sheriff Cox told the *Times-Courier*.[10]

Finally, in 1992, twelve years after the discovery of the body, there was a real break in the case. On November 20, the Sheriff's Department held another press conference in Charleston, this time to announce that the identity of the Airtight victim had been ascertained. Her name was Diana Marie Riordan-Small, a resident of Bradley, Illinois, who disappeared from her home a short time before her remains were found over 100 miles away in Coles County. The revelation was the result of cooperation between Coles County Sheriff's Detective Art Beier and Detective Steven Coy of the Bradley Police Department. Slowly but surely, a picture of what happened to Diana Small began to emerge.

The reason that no one who matched the description of the body found at Airtight turned up in the missing persons reports was that Diana was never reported missing. "Her husband... told police he wasn't all that concerned because Small had left home on occasions before," the *Journal Gazette* reported. Furthermore, Diana's mother and sister had joined a small Christian sect before moving west, where they became disconnected from Diana and her husband. After nearly a decade, her sister, Virginia, left the church and moved to North Carolina. Virginia decided to get in touch with the rest of her family and learned of her sister's disappearance, at which point she filed a missing persons report. According to Dave Fopay of the *Journal Gazette*,

"Detective Art Beier saw the report on a national listing, realized Small's descriptions matched that of the Airtight Bridge victim and contacted Bradley police."[11] A DNA test confirmed the match.

It turned out investigators early on in the case were right about one thing, the Airtight victim did have a child. Vanessa LaGessa was only two years old when her mother disappeared. Thanks to her aunt, Nicole Small, who contacted me after reading an issue of the *Legends and Lore of Illinois* I had written about the Airtight case, I recently had the pleasure of corresponding with Vanessa. She shed light on what happened after her mother's disappearance, and what her family has gone through dealing with the tragedy. Understandably, her father had no desire to discuss the incident. "I believe my dad honestly didn't know how to tell me that my mother was murdered even as I got older," she explained to the *Times-Courier* in 2008.[12]

"I am relieved that someone actually still cares enough about my mother to dig deeper into her murder," she wrote to me. "I was only two at the time. The case was reopened once in 1995 and once I talked to the detective and my dad refused to talk to him... My dad knows that the spouses are the first suspects in cases like this." Vanessa has a seven year old son, and one day she will have to explain to him what happened to his grandmother.[13]

In October 2008, the anonymous headstone that had marked the grave of Diana Small was replaced with one bearing her name. Mark Temples, who had left a flower on the grave many times over the years, never lived to see the new headstone. He died on June 10, 2007. "I am grateful for how well her [former] headstone was taken care of and it was finally nice to meet Mr. Cox the Sheriff of Coles County and some of the people who have visited her grave over the years," Vanessa said. "We have waited a long time to finally get some kind of closure... I am very grateful to you and everyone who has been involved in her case all these years."[14] Adams Memorials, who had donated the original monument, donated the new one as well.

With the laying of a new monument, this chapter of the Airtight Bridge murder comes to an end, but the family of the victim and the few who refuse to give up the pursuit of justice will never forget. After the body was found, the number of drinking parties at Airtight became few and far between, as if the discovery itself permanently scarred the land. Those rusted, burgundy trestles that span the Embarras along that narrow, winding road in rural Coles County will always elicit a tingle along the spines of visitors, as well as a supernatural sense that something very wrong happened there.

Chapter Endnotes

[1]*Daily Eastern News* (Charleston) 27 October 2005.

[2]National Register of Historic Places, "Illinois - Coles County," <http://www.national-registerofhistoricplaces.com/il/Coles/state.html> (22 May 2009).

[3]*Times-Courier* (Charleston) 21 October 1980; *Daily Eastern News* (Charleston) 27 October 2005.

[4]*Eastern News* (Charleston) 28 March 1977; *Eastern News* (Charleston) 15 April 1977.

[5]*Daily Eastern News* (Charleston) 22 October 1980; *Journal Gazette* (Mattoon) 20 October 1980.

[6]Grant C. Johnson, *Report of Coroner's Physician to the Coroner of Coles County, Illinois* (Springfield: Sangamon County Coroner's Office, 1980), 2-3.

[7]*Journal Gazette* (Mattoon) 21 October 1980; *Times-Courier* (Charleston) 22 October 1980.

[8]*Houston Chronicle* (Houston) 28 June 1998.

[9]Mark Temples, interview by author, 12 September 2006.

[10]*Times-Courier* (Charleston) 5 December 2008.

[11]*Journal Gazette* (Mattoon) 10 December 1992.

[12]*Times-Courier* (Charleston) 5 December 2008.

[13]Vanessa LaGesse "Airtight case- Vanessa Small- LaGesse," personal email (13 October 2008).

[14]Vanessa LaGesse "Re: Visit to Airtight Bridge Jane Doe," personal email (25 October 2008).

Dug Hill Road
and the
Ghost of Marshal Welch

It was dark, and Rusty had been hauling cargo from Missouri to Illinois all day. He decided to take a shortcut up Route 146 from Cape Girardeau to Interstate 57, passing through Jonesboro and Anna along the way. The terrain became rough and hilly as he turned east and began to pass through a narrow strip of the Shawnee National Forest near Hamburg Hill. As his blurry eyes scanned the horizon for any sign of the nearing town, he almost missed the black shape laying on the asphalt. He slammed on his brakes.

Someone must be playing a prank, Rusty thought as he got out of his truck. He noticed through the glare of his headlights that the shape in the road was the body of a man, who wore an outfit that looked like it had come out of a spaghetti western. It was no joke, however. As he got closer, he saw blood oozing from several wounds in the crumpled body. Just then, a motorcycle screeched to a stop in the oncoming lane.

"Is everything all right?" the biker shouted.

By the time Rusty looked up at the newcomer and back at the road, the body was gone.

For more than a century, a ghost has haunted this lonely stretch of Route 146, formerly known as "Dug Hill Road," in rustic Union County. Although sightings have become less frequent in recent years, the ghost of Provost Marshal Welch has earned an iconic place in the folklore of southern Illinois. Like many of its kind, this ghost story preserves the memory of a real event, an event that took place at a traumatic time in the history of our state and our country. But the details of this event have become murky and distorted. While Provost Marshal Welch was actually killed in 1863, every recent retelling of the tale places his murder in 1865. Also, at some point during the reprinting of the story, authors changed Route 146 to "Highway 126," which has created a very confusing state of affairs for anyone wanting to visit the location. There is no Highway 126 anywhere in Union County. Complicating matters further, a quaint country lane off Route 146 is now the only feature in the area named "Dug Hill."

The truth is that Marshal Welch was killed in the early spring of 1863 along what we now know as Illinois Route 146, a few miles west of Jonesboro past the tiny village of Berryville. The legend, however, is a different matter entirely. Storytellers generally agree that Welch died in an ambush during the waning days of the Civil War, but the details vary depending on who is doing the telling.

In one version of the ambush, a handful of Union army deserters shot and killed Welch as he headed home along Dug Hill Road. Welch had arrested the deserters and handed them over to the army a few days earlier, but since the army received word that General Lee had surrendered at Appomattox, it let them go. "Late that night, Welch was riding home and he passed through the cut alongside Dug Hill," Troy Taylor wrote. "He had no idea that the deserters were waiting for him there. They shot and killed him as he rode by and left his body lying in the road... no one was ever arrested for the crime and the mystery remained unsolved."[1]

In another version, one of a dozen deserters befriended Welch and led him into the ambush as revenge for having arrested him and his compatriots during the war. According to Beth Scott and Michael Norman, "Another of the men loaded all but two rifles with blank cartridges. The bushwhackers selected the guns at random. As Welch neared the point of ambush... he was cut down as he passed through Dug Hill below some bushes in which the men had hidden."[2]

Neither version is technically correct, but their essential features remain the same.

In order to understand the story of the unfortunate Mr. Welch and his ghost, one needs to understand the environment of southern Illinois during the 1860s. Long before there was *American Idol*, there was an American Civil War, which was fought over a number of issues, the most prominent being slavery and state's rights. The citizens of Illinois were as deeply divided over those political and economic issues as they are over the issues of today, but the disputes of the early nineteenth century were exacerbated by cultural and regional differences. When the United States won its independence in 1783, Virginia claimed most of the territory that became Illinois. As a result, many of the early pioneers of Illinois, who settled the land along the Ohio and Mississippi rivers, were from Southern states such as Virginia, Kentucky, and Tennessee, which at that time relied on slavery to drive their economy.

Consequently, Illinois entered the Union in 1818 with strict "black codes" on the books. The Illinois constitution prohibited the introduction of slavery, but permitted those residents already holding slaves to keep their property. As historian Suzanne Guasco explained, Illinois was the only state created out of the Northwest Territory that did not explicitly abolish slavery during its constitutional convention. In February 1823, the Illinois House of Representatives passed a resolution that called for a convention to revise the state constitution with the aim of legalizing the slave trade in Illinois. When the convention resolution was put to a popular vote, 57 percent of the voters, most of whom were persuaded by the argument that the induction of a slave trade would harm free white labor, rejected the resolution.[3] It was hardly a ringing endorsement of abolitionism.

In fact, abolitionists in Illinois were routinely attacked by their opponents. Elijah Lovejoy, a prominent newspaper editor and abolitionist from Missouri who moved to Illinois to escape pro-slavery partisans, had his printing press destroyed by mobs three times. He was murdered in Alton in 1837 for his views. As time went on, the Illinois electorate became politically bifurcated over how to deal with the fate of slavery in the country. In 1854, a small nucleus of Republicans led by Owen Lovejoy attempted to fuse Whigs and Free Soilers into their burgeoning party. At first, their efforts met resistance everywhere but in the northernmost counties of Illinois, then the debate over the Kansas-Nebraska Act created an opportunity for the Republican Party to replace its rivals and at the same time ended the hegemony of the Democratic Party in the state.[4]

In the 1856 election, Democratic presidential candidate James Buchanan narrowly won Illinois with a 3.86 percent margin over the popular free-labor exponent John C. Fremont. Republican William H. Bissell won the governorship with an even slimmer margin. In the 1860 presidential election, Republican Abraham Lincoln defeated Democrat Stephen A. Douglas by only 3.52 percent of the popular vote.[5]

On the eve of the election of 1860, the voters of Illinois were ideologically divided into two political camps—Democrats and Republicans—but there was a stark geographic contrast between the strongholds of the two parties. Counties in northern Illinois voted overwhelmingly Republican, and counties in southern Illinois, with the notable exception of Edwards County, voted overwhelmingly Democrat. For instance, Jackson County, a county bordering the one in which Marshal Welch was ambushed, gave 76 percent of its vote to the Democratic candidate. Between the two strongholds (where over 59.5 percent of the votes went to one party) lay a large swath of Illinois in which the voting margin narrowed considerably.

When the Southern states seceded in the winter of 1860, many in "Little Egypt" were supportive of their Southern brethren, even threatening to secede from Illinois and join the Confederacy, but when the Civil War broke out in 1861, the most vocal opponents of the Union had a change of heart. Residents of southern Illinois joined the Union army in droves. That did not, however, prevent a minority of Southern sympathizers, known as "copperheads," from acting out to obstruct the war effort.

While many Democrats, as members of the opposition party, opposed the war and the policies of the Lincoln administration generally, only a few took the next step into taking action against those policies.

Those actions included attempts to obstruct the draft, the formation of local militias, statements of support for the Confederacy or against the "criminality" of the Lincoln administration, and the encouragement of desertion, as well as the destruction of the property of Unionists and abolitionists. With the exception of a few isolated instances, such as a group of women who threw eggs at a draft enrollment official in Boone County in northern Illinois,[6] the majority of overtly belligerent activities took place not in Little Egypt, where they were most expected, but in the central region of the state.

The most dramatic incident involving copperheads and Union soldiers in Illinois during the course of the war occurred in Charleston, in Coles County on March 28, 1864, and violence soon broke out all over central Illinois. That summer, Montgomery, Fayette, and Bond counties were subjected to raids by "Confederate sympathizers" led by a man named Clingman. The west-central counties of Calhoun, Greene, Scott, Morgan, Macoupin, and Fulton all experienced disturbances that locals pointed to as examples of copperhead activity. Richland County also saw mob action against the draft. Most of these counties, with the exception of Calhoun, Greene, and Fayette, were hotly contested during the presidential election of 1860. Every one of them experienced a growth in Democratic Party support during the congressional election of 1862.[7]

Reports of Democrats arming and drilling and making threats against "abolitionists" spooked local Republicans. Brigadier General Jacob Ammen, commander of Camp Douglas in Chicago for most of 1863, received dozens of letters from Republicans either reporting disloyal acts or begging for weapons and soldiers for protection. Typical of these letters were three that described instances of disloyalty in Christian, Sangamon, and Macon counties. On April 21, 1863, Capt. A.B. Weber wrote regarding an "exhibition of disloyalty" he witnessed while passing through the town of Pana. A "squad of like sympathizers hollered for 'Jeff Davis' as they saw me pass with uniform on," he wrote. "They aught to be sent south."

From Grandview, a town located just outside of the state capital, one man wrote: "[Knights of the Golden Circle] are very numerous here and say they won't submit to a draft and are drilling here after night on some occasions."[8] A man from Niantic, located in Macon County, wrote to General Ammen to inform him that local Republicans had formed a "loyal league" to combat copperheads who were incensed over the arrest of Clement Vallandigham, an Ohio politician who was an outspoken critic of Lincoln and the war. "Lockhart [one of the copperheads] swore if they do not release their leader Vallandigham they would avenge themselves on the men that advocate the arrest of him," he wrote. "He says that in less than a month they will murder all the g—d Republicans that dare to take sides with the administration."[9]

It was in this context, in the heated spring of 1863, as General Ulysses S. Grant closed in on Vicksburg, Mississippi, that the murder of Provost Marshal Welch occurred. The ambush and subsequent murder was said to have taken place outside of Anna, one of two cities in Union County. Union County was the only county in the state of Illinois to cast a statistically significant number of ballots (40.3 percent) for the Southern Democrat candidate John C. Breckinridge in the 1860 presidential race. That meant that out of all the counties in Illinois, Union was (perhaps ironically considering its name) the most pro-Southern and pro-slavery.

On April 18, 1863, Major Curtis sent a letter to General Ammen informing him of the death of a Mr. Welch, a provost marshal who had arrested a number of Union army deserters near Anna. Anna was a much larger town than Jonesboro at the time, and would have served as their frame of reference. General Burnside, who commanded the Union garrison in Little Egypt, dispatched an order to Major Curtis that read:

"It is stated in this morning papers that a man named Welch who arrested some deserters was assaulted and killed at Anna. I desire that you will at any cost have the perpetrators arrested and sent to headquarters (at Cincinnati) for trial, with proper witnesses. Send parties sufficiently strong to do the work, with orders to shoot down any persons who may resist their authority. Let this order be executed promptly."

The general dispatched a second provost marshal who rounded up and arrested eleven "rebel sympathizers" for the crime.[10] This number may be the source of the "dozen bushwhackers" mentioned in the folkloric version of events.

Sometime after the incident, rumors began to circulate that Welch's ghost haunted the road. According to Beth Scott and Michael Norman, "the fact that the road is haunted has never been questioned."[11] In Jo-Anne Christensen's book *Ghost Stories of Illinois*, as well as in several others, a tale was told about how, during the late 1800s, a man traveling by horse-drawn wagon through Dug Hill at night happened upon a bloody body lying in the middle of the road. When he dismounted to administer aid to the stranger, he found that his hands passed through the body and clutched at the ground, as though the man wasn't even there. He tried again, with the same result. Frightened and confused, he got back into his wagon and rushed forward, "running over" the translucent corpse in the process. While some storytellers maintain he never looked back, Jo-Anne Christensen wrote, "Questioning his sanity, the traveler turned for one look back. There was nothing on the road."[12]

One additional story told about Dug Hill Road concerned a hair-raising encounter with a wagon pulled by a team of maddened horses. It is unclear whether this was associated with the Welch legend, or was of an entirely different sort. The fact is often left ambiguous by chroniclers of the area's folklore. Nevertheless, there has only been one encounter with the phantom wagon and that was documented by Charles Neely as told to him by Mr. John H. Treece, a resident of Jonesboro, during the 1930s. The story went, in part:

"Bill was a-haulin' off corn one day. It's been a long time ago. He'd hauled off three loads of corn that day and was a-goin' home after dark. He had to pass through Dug Hill for he lived in the bottoms. He'd jest about got half-way down the hill, goin' west, when the neck-yoke of one of his horses come off, and Bill had to stop the wagon right there on the grade and git out to fix the yoke...

"As Bill was down there a-fixin' the yoke, he 'eared the awfullest racket a man ever did 'ear. It sounded like some drunk man a-drivin' an empty wagon over the road as fast as the horses could go... It scared Bill to death nearly, for he knowed that there wasn't enough room for the wagon to git by on account of the road bein' so narrow, and Bill knowed he couldn't get out of the way...

"The noise was on the brink of the hill. Bill looked up, and he realized that the noise of the wagon was in the air above him and not on the road a-tall.

"Bill looked up in the air, and he seed comin' over the crest of the hill a heavy pair of black horses a-pullin' a heavy wagon a-drivin'. The horses were a-runnin' up there in the air just like they was on the ground... The wagon and team passed right over Bill's head and struck the crest of another hill, and Bill couldn't see it any more, but he 'eard the noise of the wagon after it had got two miles away!"[13]

That incredible story has been repeated in every retelling of the legend of Dug Hill since its publication. In *Ghost Stories of Illinois*, Jo-Anne Christensen conflated the story of Welch's ghost and the aerial wagon. When anyone was forced to stop along the road to fix a wagon wheel or to change a tire, she wrote, they would be greeted by the pounding of horse's hooves and the rattle of a wooden wagon. "The driver of the runaway rig has never been identified—but there are those who think it might be Provost Marshal Welch, making one last attempt to escape the fate he met on that dark night..."[14]

Today, the Dug Hill area is used as a local drinking spot. Empty beer bottles litter the woods along Route 146 in the hinterland of the Shawnee National Forest. According to former *Daily Egyptian* reporter Kristina Dailing, many who live in the area are skeptical of the stories, and many more have never even heard the tale of Provost Marshal Welch. Paul Morgan, a long time resident of Jonesboro, said he believed the stories had simply been invented. "I've heard that there was supposed to be a spook up there, but I haven't ever seen anything," he told Kristina.[15]

Perhaps this is a chapter in the history of Little Egypt destined to fade from memory.

Chapter Endnotes

[1]Troy Taylor, *Haunted Illinois: The Travel Guide to the History & Hauntings of the Prairie State* (Alton: Whitechapel Productions Press, 2004), 50.

[2]Beth Scott and Michael Norman, *Haunted Heartland: True Ghost Stories from the American Midwest* (New York: Barnes & Noble Books, 1985, 1992), 40.

[3]Suzanne Cooper Guasco, "'The Deadly Influence of Negro Capitalists': Southern Yeomen and Resistance to the Expansion of Slavery in Illinois" *Civil War History* 47 (Winter 2001): 13.

[4]William E. Gienapp, *The Origins of the Republican Party, 1852-1856* (New York: Oxford University Press, 1987), 122.

[5]Howard W. Allen and Vincent A. Lacey, eds., *Illinois Elections, 1818-1990: Candidates and County Returns for President, Governor, Senate, and House of Representitives* (Carbondale: Southern Illinois University Press, 1992), 10-11.

[6]Wood Gray, *The Hidden Civil War: The Story of the Copperheads* (New York: The Viking Press, 1942), 138.

[7]Ibid., 150-151.

[8]Carl L. Stanton, *They Called it Treason: an Account of Renegades, Copperheads, Guerrillas, Bushwhackers and Outlaw Gangs that Terrorized Illinois During the Civil War* (Bunker Hill: by the author, 2002), 88.

[9]Ibid., 92-93.

[10]Ibid., 83.

[11]Scott and Norman, 40.

[12]Jo-Anne Christensen, *Ghost Stories of Illinois* (Edmonton: Lone Pine, 2000), 30.

[13]Charles Neely, ed., *Tales and Songs of Southern Illinois* (Menasha: George Banta Publishing, 1938; reprint, Carbondale: Southern Illinois University Press, 1998), 80-81.

[14]Ibid., 31.

[15]*Daily Egyptian* (Carbondale) 22 October 2002.

Lakey's Creek
and the
Headless Horseman of Illinois

"I almost wept as the spectra placed
The head back into the sack;
Clop, clop… the headless rider
moved on."

~Neil Tracy, "The Legend of Lakey"

LaKey Creek drains the farmland northwest of the town of McLeans-boro and heads south, eventually joining the north fork of the Saline River in rural Hamilton County. From there, the Saline River grows more robust, until it ultimately empties into the Ohio River on the eastern side of the Shawnee National Forest. The creek would have been a strategic place for any early setter of McLeansboro Township. Unfortunately for Mr. Lakey, who would lend his name to the creek, the picturesque tract of land he picked for a homestead was also his place of death. For it was with his life that he purchased the immortality of having both a creek and a local legend associated with his name.

Not long after the death of Lakey, two travelers reportedly were chased by a fearsome black steed, upon which sat a headless rider. The horseman menaced them until they crossed the creek, at which point the phantom turned downstream and disappeared.

The headless horseman of Lakey's Creek is quite possibly one of the oldest ghost stories in Illinois. Passed down as an oral tradition until John W. Allen put the story on paper in 1963, the mysterious man named Lakey, as well as his untimely end, has been immortalized in the folklore of Southern Illinois. Like Jonesboro's legend of Dug Hill and Provost Marshal Welch, this story may also be preserving the memory of an unsettling event in local history.

Long before a concrete bridge spanned the shallow creek 1.5 miles east of McLeansboro along Route 14, folklorists say, a frontiersman named Lakey attempted to erect his log cabin near a ford along the wagon trail to Mt. Vernon. His task was nearly completed when he felled an oak tree to make boards for his roof. The next morning, a lone traveler stumbled upon Lakey's bloody body. Lakey's head had

been severed by his own ax, which was left imbedded in the stump of the oak. According to legend, his murderer was never found.

But the story doesn't end there.

For decades after the murder, travelers reported being chased by a headless horseman that rode out of the woods along Lakey's Creek. "Always the rider, on a large black horse, joined travelers approaching the stream from the east, and always on the downstream side," John Allen wrote. "Each time and just before reaching the center of the creek, the mistlike figure would turn downstream and disappear."[1] The headless rider descended upon travelers heading west toward McLeansboro and silently escorted them until they reached the creek. The phantom never gave any indication of a motivation for the pursuit, nor displayed any aggressiveness towards those who encountered him.

For many years, folklorists, genealogists, and local historians alike have tried to determine who gave his name to LaKey Creek, and whether this person might have also inspired the headless horseman legend. As it turns out, there is good evidence to suggest the story of the murder is true, and that the legend might be older than the town of McLeansboro or Hamilton County itself.

In 1973, Ralph S. Harrelson published research in which he claimed to have learned the historical personage behind the Lakey legend. In a history of Hamilton County, he discovered a single sentence revealing that a man named Lakey—the same man who gave his name to the creek—had indeed lived near the ford, but more tellingly, that he had been murdered by his son-in-law. The entry read, "Mr. Lakey, who lived on the Jones Tract, after whom Lakey's Creek was named, and who was killed by his son-in-law." After further research, Harrelson discovered that a man named Joel Leaky had owned a tract of land in that vicinity prior to 1824. "Leaky," apparently, was a variation in the spelling of "Lakey." "Joel could be, and probably is, the person for whom the creek is named," he concluded.[2]

The descendents of Leaky or Leakey (their surname is now spelled Lakey) have also poured through papers and documents, trying to get to the bottom of the grisly affair. They discovered that a Simon Leakey, born June 8, 1778 in Surry County, North Carolina, joined many of his Southern brethren in leaving his home and traveling north in search of cheap and profitable land. He wound up in Ohio in 1807 and then moved to Illinois in 1816. He took with him his wife, Ruth, and three children, Anna, Jacob, and Elizabeth. Two other daughters, Mary and Sarah, both died before the family reached Illinois. Simon also had a brother named Joel, who was married to a woman named Nancy Calloway. On February 7, 1817, when Illinois was still a territory and Hamilton County had not yet been created out of White County, Joel purchased a plot of land along a creek in Township 5 Range 6 NE quarter of Section 23 (Range 5 according to Ralph Harrelson). On February 18, 1817, Michael Jones, the land agent for White County, bought that same property.[3] What happened in the twelve days between the two purchases? Was that, perhaps, just enough time for Joel to erect a cabin before being brutally murdered? History tells a different story.

We know from probate records that Michael Jones took Simon Leakey to court in 1819 for trespassing on his land. The case never went to trial because, according to a Bible record (births and deaths at that time were often recorded in the family Bible), Simon died in 1819 and was buried near Lakey Creek. According to the RootsWeb entry for Joel Leakey, Simon was murdered. If the Hamilton County history book is correct, and Simon was murdered by his son-in-law, it had to have been at the hands of the husband of one of his two surviving daughters, Ann or Elizabeth. Records show that Elizabeth married in 1826, so her husband could not have done the terrible deed. Ann, however, married a man named Hiram Long in White County in either 1818 or 1819. They moved to St. Clair County, on the opposite site of the state, soon after. But if Hiram Long murdered Simon Leakey, there are no official records to prove it. Simon's wife, Ruth, moved to Lawrence County, Indiana in 1820. It was for those reasons that Gilbert M. Lakey, a descendent of the Leakeys, believed that Simon, and not Joel, was the one for whom the creek was named. Joel moved to Texas, where he died on February 25, 1837.[4] By 1820 there was no one living in White County named Leaky or Lakey.

Hamilton County split from White in 1821, and McLeansboro was platted in that same year.

The tale of the headless horseman of southern Illinois has graced the pages of many monographs on Illinois ghostlore since its first printing in 1963. Among others, Lakey's ghost has appeared in Beth Scott and Michael Norman's *Haunted Heartland* (1985), Jo-Anne Christensen's *Ghost Stories of Illinois* (2000), Troy Taylor's *Haunted Illinois* (1999, 2004), and Chad Lewis and Terry Fisk's *Illinois Road Guide to Haunted Locations* (2007).

Since it is an old ghost story without many repeat sightings, the accounts given in the aforementioned books do not show much variation. However, storytellers have added some of their own details to John Allen's original telling. In Troy Taylor's account, the man who discovered Lakey's body was a neighbor who stopped by to drop off a batch of eggs. "He knew that his friend planned to purchase some laying hens soon, but with the cabin nearly completed, there had simply not been time," he wrote. "Rounding the back of the house, he discovered Lakey's bloody and headless body beside a tree stump."[5] Jo-Anne Christensen added that Lakey, at least in legend, "had no family that anyone knew of."[6] A little creative license is rarely uncalled for in the business of ghostlore.

Although both Taylor and Christensen implied that the headless horseman has been seen in modern times, even after the concrete bridge was constructed over the creek in 1952, only Chad Lewis and Terry Fisk's work contained a contemporary encounter with the phantom. A local woman, who was familiar with the Lakey legend and who the authors kept anonymous, told them about the incident. The woman passed over the bridge every day on her way to and from work. One evening, she saw something strange in the woods. "As the woman slowed down to get a better look at what she had seen, she almost crashed her car because of what was staring back at her," Lewis and Fisk related. "Perched on top of a large horse was a man with no head."[7]

Today, a grassy field and a small wooded area cover the land where Lakey's cabin once stood. LaKey Creek still trickles and winds its way on an inexorable course south through Hamilton County. Only it and its mysterious headless rider will ever know what really happened along its muddy banks over 190 years ago.

Chapter Endnotes

[1] John W. Allen, *Legends & Lore of Southern Illinois* (Carbondale: Southern Illinois University, 1963, 1973), 59.

[2] Ralph S. Harrelson, "History and Legend of Lakey," *Goshen Trails* (October 1973): 13.

[3] Kenneth and Gilbert M. Lakey, et al., "A. W. Lakey, ID: I06655," *RootsWeb.com*, < http://wc.rootsweb.ancestry.com/cgi-bin/igm.cgi?op=GET&db=awlakey&id=I06655 > (4 June 2009).

[4] Kenneth Lakey, et al., "A. W. Lakey, ID: I07216," *RootsWeb.com*, < http://wc.rootsweb.ancestry.com/cgi-bin/igm.cgi?op=GET&db=awlakey&id=I07216> (4 June 2009).

[5] Troy Taylor, *Haunted Illinois: The Travel Guide to the History & Hauntings of the Prairie State* (Alton: Whitechapel Productions Press, 2004), 57.

[6] Jo-Anne Christensen, *Ghost Stories of Illinois* (Edmonton: Lone Pine, 2000), 226.

[7] Chad Lewis and Terry Fisk, *The Illinois Road Guide to Haunted Locations* (Eau Claire: Unexplained Research Publishing Company, 2007), 263.

The Phantom Lady
of Kennedy Hill Road

It was a few weeks before Christmas, 1980. A peanut farmer named Jimmy Carter was preparing to hand over the presidency of the United States to an actor named Ronald Reagan. The Iran hostage crisis was winding down, and the economy was weakening. That month, the national unemployment rate reached 7.2 percent. Outside the sleepy town of Byron, Illinois, the massive cooling towers of the nearby nuclear power plant were still under construction.

Kim Anderson turned down Kennedy Hill Road and headed for home after attending church early Sunday morning. Snow drifted across the country road and ice glistened on the barren fields. As her driveway neared, her mind wandered to thoughts of getting inside and cooking a hot breakfast. Without warning, she noticed a young woman, around the same age as she, walking down the road toward her driveway. The woman had long, blond hair, and strangely, wore a pair of light colored shorts. Kim pulled her car into her driveway and ran into the house. She threw open the curtains on the front room window to see if the woman was going to come up the driveway. She didn't. Instead, she continued walking toward Byron. Kim didn't think much of the encounter after that, until she began to hear the rumors.

Between mid-December and early January, dozens of people reported seeing a young woman in various stages of dress walking down Kennedy Hill Road. By January 20, 1981, the sightings had reached a fevered pitch. Wild reports circulated around Ogle County, and motorists parked their cars in the frigid temperatures along the narrow rural road to catch a glimpse of what became known as "The Phantom Lady of Kennedy Hill Road." Newspaper reports reached as far away as Chicago, and the Rockford *Register Star* ran five consecutive articles on the sightings.

Kim Anderson was one of the first to spot the scantily-clad woman, but other reports soon followed. *Register Star* correspondent Diane Moats diligently collected dozens of eyewitness accounts from what she described as "credible" regular folks, "not the kind you'd think would make up something like this." Years after the sightings, she told Bill Rowe of *Rockford Magazine*, "Each of them claimed to have seen the woman walking alongside the road. By the time they stopped to see if she was okay, she had disappeared."[1] The woman was always described as being inappropriately dressed for the weather, and occasionally barefoot. While many encounters with "the phantom" seemed down to earth, many more crossed the line from reality to fiction. At least twenty individuals with whom Diane spoke fell back on a familiar folklore motif; that of the Vanishing Hitchhiker. They told the reporter that they each knew someone who picked up the young woman and drove her home, only to find out upon arrival and after speaking with her mother that she had died years earlier. In all instances, the mysterious hitchhiker vanished from his or her car when they arrived at their destination.[2]

While those particular encounters were obviously driven by hearsay and wild speculation, the majority of sightings were simple and straight-forward. Many of the passing motorists were genuinely concerned for the young woman and turned their car around to ask her if she needed help, but she was then nowhere to be seen. For all, it was too incredible to believe. What would a living, breathing person be doing walking along the roadside in the dead of winter, and how could she just disappear? "Usually if you meet someone just walking along the road, there's a car out of commission somewhere, but there was no car on the road whatsoever," a waitress and eyewitness named Betty Lingel told the *Register Star*. "I thought it was kind of goofy, just walking down the road like that. It was cold, below zero."[3]

Dave Trenholm and his friend Guy Harrigan were driving down Kennedy Hill Road the night of January 2, just goofing off and talking about the day's events. Suddenly, a spritely young woman about 5 feet 7 inches tall jumped out of the brush along the side of the road and be-gan jogging south. Incredibly, she appeared to be barefoot and dressed only in black panties and a black scarf. "I almost wrecked my car trying to stop," Dave told reporter Diane Moats. "I thought maybe someone was in trouble and then maybe it was a gag, because it appeared to me that she jumped the fence and it must be five feet."[4]

If it was someone's idea of a joke, the Ogle County Sheriff's Depart-ment, along with some local residents, were not amused. People began to drive out to Kennedy Hill Road, sometimes bumper to bumper, hoping to see the woman. In their attempt to stay warm during the vigil, they left behind a trail of empty beer cans and candy wrappers. Sheriff's deputies patrolled the road, arrested a few people who were blocking driveways, but found no sign of a wandering woman, clothed or other-wise. "In the last three weeks we have only received three or four calls and we've investigated," Lt. James Drymiller of the Ogle County Sher-iff's Department told the local newspaper, the *Northern Ogle Tempo*. In a letter to the editor, Dave "Sick of the Phantom" Osadjan complained, "When you live on a four-mile-long country road, a road that is popu-lated by fifteen or sixteen families, the last thing that you expect is a major traffic jam... if you are planning on going 'ghost hunting' in the near future, be forewarned. The police will be on duty in the area."[5] In the latter half of January, rumors began to circulate in Byron High School that the phantom had been run over by a sheriff's patrol car. The patrolman inside allegedly heard the crunch of bones, but saw no body when he got out to investigate. The story was "preposterous," Lt. Drymiller told the *Register Star*.[6]

On the morning of Friday, January 16, a man named Steve Mc-Quewlin, claiming to be a psychic and parapsychologist for "Sonnet Corp." in Milwaukee, Wisconsin, called into WYFE Radio during the Dick Bascom show and told the disk jockey his firm was sending him to Rockford to investigate the phantom sightings. That night, McQuewlin and Bascom met the editor of the *Ogle County Life* and a reporter from the *Register Star* in Byron and headed out to Kennedy Hill. None of them saw the phantom, but after they went home empty handed, the *Register Star* reporter called Milwaukee to investigate McQuewlin's credentials. It turned out that no one in Milwaukee had ever heard of McQuewlin, Sonnet Corp., or the man he said was his boss. The *Register Star* confronted McQuewlin, and he admitted the whole thing had been a hoax. "I didn't want anyone to get hurt," he explained to Diane Moats. "You guys (the media) are making so light of the situation, I wanted to see if I could stop anyone from getting hurt."[7]

Explanations for the phantom were as diverse and as strange as the situation warranted. One of the most popular theories among local teenagers was that the phantom lady was the ghost of a woman who was buried in a nearby cemetery that had been plowed over. She now prowled the road, searching for her grave. Another explanation, put forward by Mary Elson of the *Chicago Tribune*, was that the lady was a mentally disabled girl who had gone missing from her home in Oregon, Illinois, around the same time the sightings began. "She reportedly had been seen in Rockford, but had disappeared before police arrived," the *Tribune* reported.[8] But the Kennedy Hill Phantom had been seen at various times between December 10 and January 15. How could the missing girl have survived outside on her own for that long?

A third and final theory, even more bizarre than all the rest, was that the phantom lady wasn't a lady at all. A Rockford man named Ken Rogers told Diane Moats that a friend and he had offered a ride to the "phantom" the day after Christmas. "She said 'No' and when we asked her if she was sure, she said 'yeah,'" he recalled. "My friend said it looked like she was a he, had a very rough voice and was the ugliest person he had ever seen."[9] Years later, Ms. Moats revealed that she had received threatening phone calls from a transvestite who claimed to be the one causing the disturbance. "His girlfriend had been killed in a skiing accident and after she died this guy took on the persona of the dead woman by dressing in woman's clothes and running around

Kennedy Hill Road,
outside of Byron.

outside," she explained to Bill Rowe. The man moved away in January, right around the time the sightings of the phantom stopped.[10]

The Phantom of Kennedy Hill Road was never seen again. A decade after the last sighting, Dale Kaczmarek and Howard Heim of the Chicago Ghost Research Society traveled out to Byron to investigate the story. They took pictures of the road and interviewed eyewitnesses, but found nothing. After so much time, the trail had gone cold. "I wanted to see the terrain for myself and examine possible hiding places and rule out the possibility of optical illusions," Kaczmarek wrote in his book *Windy City Ghosts*.[11]

The Phantom Lady of Kennedy Hill Road proves that folklore is continually being created. An event does not have to take place in the distant past to constitute a legend. It can have a very modern setting and even be caused by a few unusual, but very real encounters that are repeated and distorted until they take on a life of their own. The phantom may have vanished forever, but her story will live on as one of the strangest chapters in the folk history of Ogle County.

Chapter Endnotes

[1]Bill Rowe, "Was Byron's Barefoot Phantom Merely a Masquerade?" *Rockford Magazine* 11 (Fall 1996): 24-25.

[2]*Register Star* (Rockford) 20 January 1981.

[3]*Register Star* (Rockford) 15 January 1981.

[4]*Register Star* (Rockford) 16 January 1981.

[5]*Northern Ogle Tempo* (Byron) 21 January 1981; *Northern Ogle Tempo* (Byron) 28 January 1981.

[6]*Register Star* (Rockford) 20 January 1981.

[7]*Register Star* (Rockford) 17 January 1981; *Register Star* (Rockford) 18 January 1981.

[8]*Chicago Tribune* (Chicago) 22 January 1981.

[9]*Register Star* (Rockford) 20 January 1981.

[10]Rowe, 25.

[11]*Register Star* (Rockford) 16 May 1992; Dale Kaczmarek, *Windy City Ghosts: An Essential Guide to the Haunted History of Chicago* (Oak Lawn: Ghost Research Society Press, 2005), 50-51.

Cuba Road

I grew up in the northwest suburbs of Chicago, Des Plaines to be exact, home of the famous Choo Choo Restaurant, the first corporate McDonalds, and the stomping grounds of John Wayne Gacy. When my friends and I wanted a scare, we usually trekked out to Cuba Road, a lonely avenue north of the Chicago suburbs, about a good half hour drive from my home. My sister, being four years older than I, was the first person I ever heard mention the road. She had just gotten her driver's license, and like many teens, wanted to take her new found freedom somewhere thrilling. Cuba Road was such a place. It was dark and remote, filled with mansions set far back from the road, and where one never knew what was lurking around the bend. There were rumors of abandoned insane asylums, phantom cars, haunted cemeteries, and a whole host of things that went bump in the night. For added danger, a few of the more fool hardy visitors turned off their headlights to see how long they could drive along the inky black avenue before common sense, and fear, got the better of them.

Cuba Road sits nestled between the towns of Lake Zurich and Barrington, both upper and upper-middle-class retreats. The main portion of the road runs between Route 12 (Rand Road) and Route 14 (Northwest Highway) and is home to a veritable cornucopia of legends. White Cemetery, located along the western half of the road, has its spook lights. The avenue itself hosts a phantom car (or cars), a pair of spectral lovers, and a vanishing house. Rainbow Road, a side street off Cuba, had the distinction of being home to an abandoned mansion that some believed was either an old asylum or a getaway for gangsters. That building has since been torn down and the property is being redeveloped.

The ghost stories that seem to literally pour out of the mouths of visitors led famed author Ursula Bielski to proclaim, "For Chicagoland ghosthunters, Cuba Road is the single most notorious haunted site north of southwest suburban Bachelors Grove Cemetery."[1] Those familiar with the notoriety of Bachelor's Grove understand the challenge of filling shoes of that size. Scott Markus, who has done impeccable research on the folklore of the road, dubbed it "the Archer Avenue of the North

Cuba Road.
Photo by the author.

Side," because of the variety of stories, and Dale Kaczmarek called White Cemetery, "the most haunted location on the north side."[2]

The road and cemetery, however, are located in Lake County, and the residents there do not consider themselves a part of Chicago or its suburbs, which are located in Cook County. The Barrington zip code, 60010, is the seventh wealthiest in the entire United States, when considering areas that filed more than 20,000 tax returns in 2008. It is rivaled only by Hinsdale, Illinois, and five zip codes in New York.[3] The economic disparity between Barrington and a suburb like Des Plaines adds to the allure of Cuba Road, since many of its visitors have a profound sense that they are intruding in a world in which they are not entirely welcome. It is a kind of reverse "slumming." Needless to say, area residents, who came there for the purpose of finding privacy, do not appreciate that their front yards have been turned into a paranormal playground.

Ela Road and Cuba Road

Our tour of Cuba Road begins at the intersection of Rand Road, where gas stations and mini malls have grown up to nearly obscure the entrance to the notorious avenue. Turning west, the first landmark to appear is the Cuba Marsh Forest Preserve. During the day, the marsh is a popular spot for cyclists, roller bladers, and joggers, but at night it takes on an eerie quality. It is the first sign that visitors have left the safe confines of the suburbs. There are no streetlights there, only the drone of insects and the croaking of frogs and other amphibians that inhabit the marsh. Some motorists attempting to find a shortcut through the marsh have gotten more than they bargained for along Ela Road.

Ela Road cuts through the Forest Preserve and heads north and south, intersecting with Cuba Road a little over a mile from Route 12. According to Rachel Brooks, author of *Chicago Ghosts*, an old barn sat along Ela Road somewhere south of Cuba. There was a swing set near the barn, she claimed, and the spirit of a young girl has been heard laughing and playing—sometimes crying—in the shadow of the dilapidated building. While there is currently no barn along Ela Road, there have been farms there in the past, and there are abandoned entrances that once led to those farms. Like many legends, the story of the red barn of Ela Road might be the last vestige of a memory of such a place.

In *Chicago Ghosts*, Rachel told the story of David, a young man who, along with a few friends, decided to explore Ela Road, but found himself unnerved by the presence of the marsh, thick with trees, on either side of the street. It was dark, and it looked like the road might go on forever. Determined to turn around and continue their trek down Cuba Road, David found what he thought was a driveway. "He pulled the car into the driveway and prepared to back out when he noticed a child's wagon sitting in the driveway near the rear of his vehicle," Ms. Brooks wrote. The disembodied laughter of a child followed the odd appearance of the toy, and David and his friends wasted no time in leaving.[4]

Cuba Road and Rainbow Road

Continuing along Cuba Road, with the Cuba Marsh Forest Preserve on the left, you will come to railroad tracks. Approximately 800 feet beyond these tracks sits Rainbow Road. Rainbow Road winds its way north through a wooded residential area populated by the wealthy and reclusive. The road turns sharply to the left, continues on, and then turns sharply right. A stone wall and a wrought iron gate formerly sat on the outside of the second curve. Behind that gate was a blacktop driveway that led deep into a grove of willow trees that obscured an old, abandoned mansion. The property was littered with buildings, a pond, a silo, and even a dog house. According to Scott Markus, the former owners of the mansion left in a hurry. "The closets still contained clothes, and the kitchen drawers still held silverware," he wrote in *Voices from the Chicago Grave*. One woman with whom he spoke described rooms full of toys, and satanic markings and animal skulls in the basement.[5] In *Haunted Illinois*, Troy Taylor claimed that trespassers witnessed lights in the windows, "strange figures," and "moaning and crying sounds."[6]

Some of the more imaginative visitors brought back stories that the building was a former insane asylum or sanitarium. For someone who never saw the property itself, or who had limited knowledge of local history, it would have been easy to believe these rumors. Many did, but in fact there never was an asylum along Rainbow Road, only this decaying old house, which was more than enough to ensure its place in local legend. Sometime in the early 2000s, the local fire department intentionally burned down the old house, but according to Mr. Markus, a guest house, tennis courts, and a barn remained. Recently, the property was redeveloped as Kaitlin's Way, "Barrington's Finest Custom Home Neighborhood." As of 2007, the old silo still stood next to one of the brand new mansions.

In his research, Scott Markus uncovered much information about the property, including an account of a tragic accident that claimed the life of a young boy. As it turned out, the owner of the mansion was a real estate developer named Robert Krilich. Mr. Krilich employed a full-time groundskeeper who looked after the property and whose family, the Cokenowers, lived in the guest house. Scott spoke with the daughter of the groundskeeper, Sherry Cokenower-Mitchell, who related the story of how, in 1968, a stone birdbath struck and killed her brother William as he attempted to climb it. He was seven years old at the time of the accident. Apparently, the ghost of a boy in a red shirt and overalls has been seen along Cuba Road, and William's father believes it might be the spirit of his long deceased son.[7]

There was another abandoned home in the area, this one less notorious. It was formerly located kitty-corner from Rainbow Road, tucked in Cuba Marsh. "Kids used to drive up there before the road was closed and neck and drink beer," a local librarian named Dorothy told Dale Kaczmarek. This house was torn down some time ago, but its driveway and foundation remain.[8]

Specters of the Past

Cuba Road is haunted by a third house, this one of a more metaphysical nature. Somewhere between the intersection of Cuba and Route 59 (Hough Street) and White Cemetery, passing motorists have caught a glimpse of a simple farmhouse—occasionally engulfed in flames— only to have it mysteriously vanish on their return trip. In *Chicago's Street Guide to the Supernatural*, Richard T. Crowe appeared to link this phantom house to the house in Cuba Marsh. "Debris from the house was still visible in the early 1980s," he wrote. "On rainy, overcast days or stormy nights one can see… an apparition, a ghostly house where once the real physical house had existed."[9]

Wherever its location, the lore is pretty clear that this house burned down, possibly with its owner inside. According to both Ursula Bielski and Rachel Brooks, an elderly woman has been spotted wandering the yard. In Rachel's account, the woman carried a lantern while she walked. "But should you try to approach the old woman or walk down the path to the house, all will be gone," she added.[10]

The mystery houses of Cuba Road, both real and imagined, bring to light a disturbing history of which most are unaware. While the stories of gangsters roaming the Barrington area, dumping bodies and doing the things wise guys do, inhabit in the murky past, there were times in recent memory when terror filled the homes along this secluded avenue. Murder occasionally left behind the abandoned properties that littered the road, and teens drank and fooled around oblivious to the violence that occurred right under their noses.

In early August 1972, a group of black Vietnam veterans, who had been dishonorably discharged, slaughtered millionaire Paul Corbett, his wife, step daughter, and sister-in-law in their Barrington Hills mansion around four miles southwest of Cuba Road. The gang called themselves De Mau Mau, after the Mau Mau uprising of Kenyans against British colonial rule from 1952 to 1960.[11]

On October 16, 1972, a nineteen-year-old girl was found dead of a gunshot wound in the bedroom of her father's home, which was located in a wooded area near the intersection of Route 59 and Cuba Road. Still nervous over the deaths of the Corbetts, local residents panicked. According to the *Chicago Tribune*, Lake County Sheriff Orville Clavey "warned reporters on the scene not to approach houses because many Barrington area residents are heavily armed." Tragically, it was that precaution that led to the death of the teenage girl. Her family had stockpiled over a dozen rifles and handguns in their home, and the girl's twelve-year-old brother found a .38 pistol, tripped, and accidentally shot and killed her.[12]

White Memorial Cemetery

A few yards beyond Route 59, not far from where that tragedy unfolded, sits the most frequently visited spot along Cuba Road: White Memorial Cemetery. There would, arguably, be no other legends along the road if it wasn't for the alluring power of this cemetery, which was the first to attract the attention of curiosity seekers and paranormal enthusiasts alike.

White Cemetery is one of the oldest burial grounds in Lake County. It dates back to 1820, when Barrington's mighty mansions were nothing more than farmer's fields or untamed wilderness. Like many other cemeteries in Illinois, this one developed a reputation during the 1960s as a place to get drunk, smoke pot, and "just be." Not all the activity at the cemetery was harmless fun, however. According to Dale Kaczmarek, in 1968, vandals spray painted swastikas on many of the headstones and knocked down many more.[13] The vandalism led to the cemetery being locked up at night, but as it can be seen clearly from the road, that hasn't prevented the curious from trying to catch a glimpse of the mysterious, white balls of light that are said to hover around the burial ground. In *More Chicago Haunts*, Ursula Bielski claimed that "luminescent figures" have occasionally accompanied these spook lights.[14]

Strange things continue to happen there to this day. In April 1993, vandals carried a headstone out of White Cemetery and left it on Cuba Road. A passing car struck the stone, but the driver wasn't injured. In the summer of 2001, I found a pile of chicken bones in the cemetery, and the previous spring several trespassers overturned and broke several gravestones.[15] The ongoing vandalism led Cuba Township officials to take extreme measures to protect the cemetery. "The nuisance has gotten so bad that township officials have permanently locked the gates," the *Chicago Tribune* reported. "The only people allowed in are family members, who are given a gate key." Area residents have also voiced their frustration. "Every time we get some press, some wacko climbs in his car convinced he can see a ghost at midnight," Tom Gooch, a longtime resident of Barrington, told the *Tribune*.[16]

Romance on Cuba Road

More than one author of Chicagoland ghostlore has noted that a romantic couple has been seen strolling along the road near the cemetery. Sometimes making an appearance in the summer, sometimes in the fall, the two walk hand in hand into the sunset before ultimately vanishing on the horizon.[17] According to Scott Markus, it is not the actual people, but their shadows that eyewitnesses spot.[18] One possible explanation for the vanishing lovers is that, while driving due west into the setting sun, a person's vision can become obstructed, even blinded, by its orange glare. It is certainly possible for a couple on an afternoon walk to disappear from sight as a result of the sun reflecting in a review mirror, or shining directly through the front windshield.

Phantom Vehicles

The phantom cars and passengers reported along the section of Cuba Road between Route 59 and Northwest Highway are slightly more difficult to explain. Some motorists have reported glancing in their rearview mirror, only to be startled by the appearance of a burly man dressed in 1920s attire, puffing on a Cuban cigar. Others swear they have been tailgated by a truck or a black car that shines its headlights into their rear windshield.[19] Rumors that Cuba Road and Lake County were a vacation destination for the likes of Al Capone are the stage upon which stories of these vanishing cars are set. For instance, a woman named Julie told Scott Markus that around ten years ago an eighteen-wheeler followed her down Cuba Road for a short distance before it abruptly disappeared. Interpreting her experience in the context of Prohibition era gangsterism, Markus speculated, "If one were to attempt to link this back to a Mafia presence, one theory could be bootlegging trucks shipping goods to a safe storage area away from the tough Chicago police."[20] The leap from vanishing automobile to the Sopranos is a natural one for an active imagination steeped in the particular history of this part of Illinois.

Railroad Crossing

Our tour of Cuba Road ends at the railroad tracks across the intersection of Route 14, approximately a mile and a half west of White Cemetery. Like the other landmarks along Cuba Road, unusual activity has been reported at this railroad crossing. Sometimes, motorists will notice an oncoming train and stop in front of the warning gates. The gates do not come down, however, and the train never arrives.[21] Other times, the warning gates will come down, but the train never comes. This phenomenon could be explained by malfunctioning warning signals, if not for the haunting train whistle that is said to accompany the strange events.

Past the railroad tracks, Cuba Road makes a few haphazard turns and ends at Plumtree Road. From Rand to Northwest Highway, Cuba Road is five miles of asphalt that has burned its way into the folk-consciousness of Illinois. For the young adults of northern Cook County, this road has become just as much a rite of passage as Archer Avenue has been for those of the south and southwestern Chicago suburbs. Residents of unincorporated Barrington may not welcome these interlopers, but as long as local teens seek out adventure along this secluded route far from the safety of city lights, they will have to bear the notoriety.

A sign warns visitors at the gate of White Cemetery.
Photo by the author.

Chapter Endnotes

[1]Ursula Bielski, *More Chicago Haunts: Scenes from Myth and Memory* (Chicago: Lake Claremont Press, 2000), 157.

[2]Scott Markus, *Voices from the Chicago Grave: They're Calling. Will You Answer?* (Holt: Thunder Bay Press, 2008), 75; Dale Kaczmarek, *Windy City Ghosts: An Essential Guide to the Haunted History of Chicago* (Oak Lawn: Ghost Research Society Press, 2005), 70.

[3]"100 wealthiest zip codes in the United States," *Wealth in the United States*, < http://wealth.mongabay.com/tables/100_wealthiest_zip_codes-20000.html> (29 May 2009).

[4]Rachel Brooks, *Chicago Ghosts* (Atglen: Schiffer Books, 2008), 113-114.

[5]Markus, 86-87.

[6]Troy Taylor, *Haunted Illinois: The Travel Guide to the History & Hauntings of the Prairie State* (Alton: Whitechapel Productions Press, 2004), 215.

[7]Markus, 89.

[8]Kaczmarek, 71.

[9]Richard T. Crowe, *Chicago's Street Guide to the Supernatural* (Oak Park: Carolando Press, 2000, 2001), 166.

DUE TO VANDALISM, THE CEMETERY IS LOCKED. WE APOLOGIZE FOR THE INCONVENIENCE. PLEASE CALL 847-381-1924 FOR ACCESS.

[10]Bielski, 158; Brooks, 113.
[11]"De Mau Mau," *Time Magazine*, 30 October 1972.
[12]*Chicago Tribune* (Chicago) 17 October 1972; *Chicago Tribune* (Chicago) 18 October 1972.
[13]Kaczmarek, 70.
[14]Bielski, 157.
[15]*Chicago Tribune* (Chicago) 2 April 1993; *Chicago Tribune* (Chicago) 23 May 2000.
[16]*Chicago Tribune* (Chicago) 7 November 2005.
[17]Bielski, 158.
[18]Markus, 79-80.
[19]Bielski, 158; Crowe, 166.
[20]Markus, 77.
[21]Kaczmarek, 71; Markus, 80.

The Abandoned

Manteno State Hospital and the "Manteno Madness"

"It is not by confining one's neighbor that one is convinced of one's own sanity."

~Fyodor Dostoyevsky

Novels (and the films based on them) such as *The Snake Pit* (1946), *One Flew Over the Cuckoo's Nest* (1962), and even memoirs like *Girl, Interrupted* (1993) have permanently colored public perception of mental hospitals. Images of sadistic Nurse Ratched and torture disguised as treatment have horrified us for decades, but those of us who grew up after the closure of such facilities have no memory of the very real scandals that led to their condemnation. At one time, Illinois had eleven state mental hospitals, located in Alton, Anna, Chicago, Dixon, East Moline, Elgin, Jacksonville, Kankakee, Lincoln, Manteno, and Peoria. Manteno State Hospital was the largest of these, and perhaps the one that attracted the most negative press. Ironically, hospitals like Manteno, with their "cottage system" of patient housing, were meant to correct the appalling conditions of what we now know as the classic "mad house" or "insane asylum" that Michel Foucault deconstructed in his influential book *Madness and Civilization* (1965). Progressive hospitals like Manteno State proved not to be much better than their predecessors, and the Community Mental Health Act of 1963 began the long, slow process of deinstitutionalization that eventually led to their closure.

It was difficult to find uses for the remains of these sprawling institutions, and most of them sat abandoned for decades. Rumors of rusted electroshock therapy beds, secret tunnels, messages left on walls by patients, and other horrors led the curious to break into old mental hospitals in search of a good scare. Some of these trespassers came back with stories of strange noises, cold drafts, and apparitions. The nature of Manteno State Hospital almost guaranteed that ghost stories would begin to spread among those adventurous enough to peer inside. There were certainly enough reasons for ghosts to haunt those halls, both literally and figuratively. Manteno State had a long history of tragedy and disgrace that reached the highest echelons of Illinois' medical community. It began with what *Time* magazine called the "Manteno Madness," a typhoid epidemic that killed more than fifty and brought down Archibald Leonard Bowen, the state director of public welfare. It ended in scandal, with charges of illicit sex and medical malpractice involving patients and staff.

Manteno State Hospital was built on 1,000 acres of land in Kankakee County, a few miles east of the village of Manteno. Construction occurred in stages over a period of several years, beginning in 1929. The hospital's diagnostic building was designed in 1931 by Chicago architectural firm Granger & Bollenbacher, with O. Herrick Hammond supervising its planning and construction. The Chicago *Daily Tribune* described its architecture as "a Georgian adaptation in face brick and Bedford stone." Manteno State's cottages originally accommodated up to 5,000 patients and included everything needed for a self-contained community. Service tunnels connected all of the buildings. From a meager 100 patients and 15 staff members in December 1930, the population at the hospital quickly ballooned to its full compliment, and the State of Illinois transferred Dr. Ralph T. Hinton from his post at Elgin State Hospital to head the new facility. By 1939 Manteno boasted 5,385 patients and 760 employees. Because most of the patients housed there weren't deemed dangerous, the hospital lacked basic security like a perimeter fence. As a result, patients occasionally escaped and alarmed the nearby community. On July 22, 1939, four patients ran away and one made it all the way into Chicago before being apprehended.[1] In 1976-1977 alone, 336 inmates escaped, but most were recaptured within three days.

The embarrassment of having so many escapees from Manteno State paled in comparison to the scandal that accompanied the typhoid epidemic of autumn 1939. Typhoid fever, once a leading cause of death, had been largely eradicated by the time the hospital opened. Therefore, in late August when patients began to get sick, orderlies believed the cause to be nothing more than an outbreak of common dysentery (diarrhea) and reported it as such to the state Board of Health. Welfare Director A. L. Bowen was suspicious, however, and ordered Manteno's well water to be chlorinated (which kills the typhoid bacteria) and sent a shipment of typhoid vaccine. By the beginning of October, between 385 and 390 patients and staff had come down with the disease, which causes fever, delirium, and dehydration. Fifty-one had died. By October 15, that number had risen to fifty-five.

When the nurses and staff at Manteno finally recognized the outbreak for what it was, panic set in. According to *Time* magazine, "Patients lay moaning in bed. Others, whipped by mad fear, beat against the screened windows, [and] grappled with attendants. Some of the attendants fell ill. All were panicky. Every night kitchen boys and or-

Manteno State Hospital.
Photo by the author.

derlies disappeared."[2] Between forty-five and fifty employees deserted their posts during the crisis, but most stayed on, working long hours to stem the tide of new infections. At the inquest into the epidemic, an attendant named Mary Burrell, who was hired as a replacement after some of the staff fled or were stricken with fever, recalled conditions at the hospital. "The patients were all excited or excitable. Many had to be restrained," she told prosecutors. "The hospital was not prepared for such an emergency. There was a deplorable lack of facilities for sanitary purposes. Neither the sick nor their bed clothing could be kept clean or properly sterilized."[3]

A leaking sewer was suspected as the cause of the epidemic. Manteno State drew its water from an underground well, which was located in limestone and was unusually close to the surface. The hospital's sewer lines were tile, and any leaks in their joints could have allowed sewage to seep through cracks in the limestone and contaminate the water supply. While both Director Bowen and Dr. Hinton pledged to fix the obvious flaws in Manteno's water and sewage system, Mr. Bowen praised the hospital staff for their efficiency and dedication. In a letter to State Representative Robert J. Branson, he wrote, "The fact that the total number of cases has been held to within 6 per cent of the total population of 6,250 is proof that the medical, nursing, and sanitation forces have done a very good job."[4]

Many were not convinced, and a report that the hospital received prior warnings about the vulnerability of its water supply provoked outrage. "The fact that the limestone that lies close to the surface at Manteno is an ideal substance for carrying sewage and surface drainage into wells is probably known to every competent plumber in that neighborhood," an editorial in the *Daily Tribune* opined. "But it was ignored by the political authorities who built the hospital... Although Manteno houses thousands of persons incapable of caring for themselves, it apparently never had occurred to the officials in charge, or their superiors in Springfield, that such a population might suffer an epidemic." The editorial alleged that public health officials tried to cover up warnings they received in regards to the sewage, as well as their own carelessness and misdiagnosis in the initial stages of the epidemic. Furthermore, the immunization ordered by Director Bowen came too late, since immunization only prevented the disease and did nothing for those already infected. "All this is none the less shocking from the fact that it is what might be expected in a system of state institutions in which employees are beholden to politics for their jobs and shaken down for political funds," the editorial concluded.[5]

Kankakee County State's Attorney Samuel Shapiro, who would later become governor in 1968, was not convinced by Bowen and Hinton's assurances either. In mid-October, he began an inquiry into the epidemic after reading a June report that alleged Manteno was the only state mental hospital not to immunize its inmates from either typhoid or smallpox. The *Daily Tribune* reported that Dr. Hinton said "it was news to him" if patients in other institutions were vaccinated against typhoid. The apparent cluelessness of health officials fanned the flames of scandal, and by the morning of October 23, the headlines cried, "REVEAL MANTENO WARNINGS." Henry Horner, then governor of Illinois, held a press conference at Manteno State, where 340 still suffered from the disease. The governor was "gravely concerned" about the situation, he said, especially after reports had come out the night before revealing that inspectors had issued several warnings about Manteno's polluted wells over the previous eight years. The reports were ignored, according to the *Daily Tribune*, because "Neither A.L. Bowen, state director of public welfare and as such head of 28 state institutions, nor Dr. Ralph T. Hinton, managing director of the Manteno institution, knew how to interpret the scientific reports when they received them." After wondering aloud why he should produce documents that could be used as evidence to indict him, Mr. Bowen finally threw up his hands and released them after being told the state's attorney could use his authority to make the documents public. Among those papers was a report by a bacteriologist that some of the water he sampled on April 27, 1939 was unsafe to drink. State Representative Leo D. Crowley immediately called for a legislative investigation.[6]

In late October, State's Attorney Samuel Shapiro began questioning physicians at Manteno. Throughout the first two weeks of November, a grand jury heard testimony from nurses, attendants, and other employees, including Fred Brackenbush, Dr. Hinton's secretary, who had to be wheeled before the jury from an isolation ward where he was still recovering from typhoid fever.[7] At the end of the testimony, the grand jury indicted four public health officials for malfeasance: Director Bowen, Dr. Hinton, Assistant Managing Officer Dr. D. Louis Steinberg, and Mrs. Lillian Williams, a dietitian. A. L. Bowen's trial began on February 13, 1940 and dragged on for two weeks before the jury—after deliberating for ninety-six hours—could not reach a verdict. Judge James V. Bartley, who oversaw the proceedings, ordered a new trial to begin immediately.[8] While Director Bowen awaited retrial, three more Manteno patients died of typhoid and two more displayed symptoms. This time, polluted water could not be blamed, since the hospital's water supply had been filtered and chlorinated after the first outbreak.[9]

Bowen's second trial began on May 13, and Judge Bartley found him guilty of negligence on June 27. "The evidence in this case shows beyond all reasonable doubt that the defendant...paid no attention whatever to the reports of the department of health," Judge Bartley told the court. "The defense adopted the theory that the epidemic was caused by a patient in the institution. I do not believe this patient had anything whatever to do with the epidemic." The charges against Dr. Hinton and Mrs. Williams were dismissed. Dr. Edward Ross replaced Dr. Hinton as head of Manteno State Hospital, and Bowen was removed as state director of public welfare. Later, the Illinois Supreme Court overturned Bowen's conviction because, the justices argued, the state's attorney failed to adequately prove his case at the second trial.[10]

For the next twenty-six years, life proceeded in Manteno State as normally as could be expected for a mental hospital. Because of Manteno's particular design, inmates were housed in large, open rooms rather than in their own individual rooms. Inside the "cottages," of which there were dozens for both men and women, there was very little privacy. It is difficult to imagine how those confined there were supposed to recover. Overcrowding at all the state hospitals was a major problem, and beds were jammed as many as could fit in any particular room. Although Manteno was the largest institution in the state, in 1946 it had a population of 6,509 persons, while it had a bed capacity of 6,303. Manteno's problem with overcrowding was relatively minor when compared with Illinois' ten other institutions. Elgin State Hospital, for example, had space for 3,844 beds but was teaming with a population of 5,204.[11] This overcrowding, which effected hospitals all over the country, was one of the catalysts behind the Community Mental Health Act of 1963. That legislation paved the way for smaller, community based care for some patients, while others were simply turned out onto the street.[12]

The year 1966 was a bad time for Manteno State Hospital. In early autumn, a labor dispute led to allegations of sexual misconduct. On September 7, 200 off-duty employees began a six-day picket outside the gates, leading Illinois Governor Otto Kerner to open an investigation into conditions at the institution. Employees alleged that a staff shortage, which included physicians, psychiatrists, nurses, and dietitians, was impairing their ability to keep Manteno running under proper standards. According to the *Chicago Tribune*, mental health institutions in Illinois had to begin hiring personnel as "institution workers" rather than civil servants because it was "impossible to find the necessary number of persons who can pass the civil service examinations for psychiatric aids." The shortage of workers, but not inmates, caused other problems. Father Joseph Donahue, Manteno's Catholic chaplain, reportedly witnessed patients engaging in sexual liaisons. He told the *Tribune* that he was "extremely upset at the mental health department's 'anything goes' philosophy."[13]

On September 15, Rabbi Harry Simon and Reverend F. T. Czerwionka, also employed as chaplains at the hospital, joined Father Donahue in accusing Zone Director Bernard Rubin, who oversaw Manteno State and two other institutions, of encouraging the illicit sexual activity. Eighteen months earlier, Rubin had abolished the segregation of men and women at the three hospitals in his district. According to Father Donahue, some female patients had been raped and others were illegally given birth control pills. He told the *Tribune*, "One doctor told me he was visiting a ward and a girl was there for the first day, filled with fear. Five different men tried to have intercourse with her... If that was my mother or sister, how would I feel?" Simon, Donahue, and Czerwionka called on the governor to appoint an impartial committee to investigate the allegations.[14]

Two days later, the Board of Mental Health Commissioners held a closed-door hearing on the matter and heard testimony by Manteno staff as well as the chaplains. Some of the employees called Father Donahue's allegations "exaggerated," while Donahue presented notarized affidavits regarding sex acts on the hospital golf course that he had personally witnessed. Dr. Bernard Rubin, for his part, denied the charges and said they were "irresponsible." Three years later, after several elderly patients were found dead in nearby cornfields, Father Donahue renewed his complaints, this time alleging abuse of the patients by orderlies and other staff. John Briggs, director of the Illinois Mental Health Department, fired Father Donahue that December, prompting a lawsuit. Adding to the embarrassment, a report by the Mental Health Department said Manteno was "plagued with problems, deficiencies, and potential crises." In regards to accusations of sexual improprieties and patient abuse, however, it said, "In no single instance did these [accusations] appear to be well founded or factual. The tragedies recounted are inherent in all psychiatric treatment efforts."[15]

In 1979, allegations of "unnecessary surgery" surfaced against physicians employed at Manteno State, prompting Cook County Public Guardian Patrick T. Murphy to call for an investigation. The controversy stemmed from a Mental Health Department memo from 1977 that quoted a psychiatrist from the University of Chicago named Dr. Patti Tighe. Dr. Tighe had wondered whether too many mastectomies and gall bladder operations had been performed at the mental hospital. "The memo suggested that surgeons in training might be doing the operations to practice their skills when less radical treatment could be employed," Jon Van of the *Chicago Tribune* reported. Upon reading the memo, Dr. Tighe immediately retracted her comments and claimed they had been misrepresented. A spokesperson for the University of Chicago admitted that some experimental surgery had been performed on inmates in Manteno State during the 1950s and '60s, but "denied that the practice was widespread."[16] Although none of these allegations were proven to be true, the allegations alone were enough to color public perception of the institution.

Beginning in the 1970s, patients were slowly transferred away from Manteno State Hospital and into Elgin Mental Health Center, nursing homes, or group homes. On December 31, 1985, the hospital closed its doors. Part of the grounds became a veterans home. Some of the "cottages" were sold to businesses and became the Illinois Diversatech Campus. Others sat abandoned and vandals broke windows and sprayed graffiti. At some point, the former mental hospital became a beacon for people interested in ghosts and hauntings, as well as those with more nefarious intentions. The Bowen Building, named after A. L. Bowen, was one of the most popular to explore because it was one of the larger buildings and contained the main offices and morgue. It was torn down in the winter of 2001, but not before photographer and artist Kristyn Vinikour shot a series of photos there called "The Gennie Messages," allegedly based on the experiences of one female patient named Gennie. Her photographs, which feature haunting images of a model posing as Gennie juxtaposed with quotations painted on the walls and on the model's body, can be viewed online at The Manteno Project.[17]

While throughout its history patients at Manteno State Hospital frequently tried to escape, a new generation of men and women are desperate to find their way inside. Accounts of ghostly sounds and encounters have filtered down from those adventurous—or fool hearty—enough to explore the old tunnels and buildings. One account, related to Troy Taylor by a female friend, involved an eerie auditory experience she won't soon forget. "She and some of her companions were walking through one of the buildings when they heard a chilling sound—the sound of a doctor being paged over the intercom system!" Taylor wrote.[18] But this is not the only strange story. In 2005, a member of a Will County "ghost hunters" group photographed a "phantom image" in one of the hospital rooms. Her colleague also claimed to record EVPs during that excursion. EVP stands for "Electronic Voice Phenomenon," a term coined by those who believe that voices of the dead can be captured on recording devices. Skeptics maintain the phenomenon is nothing more than static, wishful thinking, or outright fraud. Nevertheless, the Will County ghost hunters insisted what they captured on film and on tape was real.[19]

Chad Lewis, who has investigated and written about many allegedly haunted locations around the Midwest, claimed the former pharmacy at Manteno State was the "most active" building in the institution when it came to the paranormal. "Over the years, I have had many reports of people who entered the old buildings and saw nurses and doctors and even patients still dressed in their gowns," he told the Kankakee Daily Journal.[20]

Although the ruins of several other state mental hospitals are rumored to be haunted, Manteno remains the most nefarious. Its future is uncertain. Only a few of its "cottages" are still abandoned, and the worst of these has been slated for demolition. A housing development called Fairway Oaks Estates now occupies a large portion of the northeast quarter of the former hospital grounds. Children play on manicured lawns in the shadow of the Neo-Georgian red-brick buildings, while sprinklers shower them with the same water enjoyed by Manteno's inmates for nearly sixty-six years. Someday soon, faded photographs and stories of phantoms will be all that remains of Manteno State Hospital.

Chapter Endnotes

[1]Asylum Projects, "Manteno State Hospital," 21 April 2009 <http://www.asylumprojects.org/tiki-index.php?page=Manteno+State+Hospital> (29 June 2009); *Daily Tribune* (Chicago) 27 December 1931; *Daily Tribune* (Chicago) 23 July 1939.

[2]"Manteno Madness," *Time*, 23 October 1939.

[3]*Daily Tribune* (Chicago) 2 November 1939.

[4]*Daily Tribune* (Chicago) 4 October 1939.

[5]*Daily Tribune* (Chicago) 19 October 1939. Apparently not much has changed in Illinois in the past 70 years.

[6]*Daily Tribune* (Chicago) 16 October 1939; *Daily Tribune* (Chicago) 23 October 1939.

[7]*Daily Tribune* (Chicago) 16 November 1939.

[8]*Daily Tribune* (Chicago) 23 November 1939; *Daily Tribune* (Chicago) 27 February 1940.

[9]*Daily Tribune* (Chicago) 17 April 1940.

[10]*Daily Tribune* (Chicago) 28 June 1940; *Daily Journal* (Kankakee) 31 March 2007.

[11]*Daily Tribune* (Chicago) 3 July 1946.

[12]See: David A. Rochefort, *From Poorhouses to Homelessness: Policy Analysis and Mental Health Care* (Westport: Auburn House, 1997).

[13]*Chicago Tribune* (Chicago) 10 September 1966.

[14]*Chicago Tribune* (Chicago) 16 September 1966.

[15]*Chicago Tribune* (Chicago) 18 September 1966; *Chicago Tribune* (Chicago) 6 February 1970.

[16]*Chicago Tribune* (Chicago) 14 April 1979.

[17]Kristyn Vinikour, The Manteno Project, "The Gennie Messages," <http://www.mantenostatehospital.com/gennie/index.html> (2 July 2009).

[18]Troy Taylor, *Haunted Illinois: The Travel Guide to the History & Hauntings of the Prairie State* (Alton: Whitechapel Productions Press, 2004), 242-243.

[19]*Daily Journal* (Kankakee) 31 October 2008.

[20]Ibid.

Independence Grove and "Devil's Gate"

A campfire crackled deep in the Independence Grove Forest Preserve north of Libertyville. Charity, Travis, Wade, and Katrina sat on thick branches around the glowing embers of the fire. Chatty and nervous, they knew they weren't supposed to be there, but they hoped they were deep enough in the forest that no one would see them. They spoke in low whispers. Far above their heads, tangled branches interrupted the silhouette of the waning moon while hushed laughter echoed from their campsite on the east bank of the Des Plaines River. Earlier in the evening, they had explored the woods along the equestrian trail and came across cement foundations, broken bottles, rusted playground equipment, and old fire hydrants where they had been told nothing like that should be. They could hardly contain their excitement.

Katrina hushed her friends. When they finally settled down, she began to tell the tale of "Devil's Gate." They had all heard rumors about the gate and the nearby woods, but Katrina promised them the *real* story. "I heard it from my uncle, who heard it from a guy who knew someone who was there," she said.

"It was the 1950s, and at that time this whole area was the property of an exclusive all-girls school. The elite of Libertyville—doctors, lawyers, politicians—all sent their daughters there. Unbeknownst to them, a dangerous man had recently been hired as one of the school's janitors. They should have paid more attention to who swept the halls and took out their trash, because this particular man had been spurned by the wife of a local politician, whose daughter now attended the school. It had been years since the incident, but this man would never forget the pain he felt. He swore revenge, not just on the politician, but on all the village's elite who had treated him like dirt.

"Finally, on a particularly black night, the man carried out his sadistic plan. Using his janitor's keys, he unlocked the doors to the girl's dorm, and one by one, lured six of the girls outside. Under cover of a cluster of pine trees, he butchered each one. He cut off their heads and hung them from the spikes of the gate at the entrance to the school. His grisly work completed, he hitchhiked out of Libertyville and was never seen again. The next morning, the other janitors discovered the horrifying scene. The school was immediately closed, and rather than cope with the tragedy, the elite of Libertyville hushed it up and expunged all memory of that place. After a short time, the iron gate was the only thing left standing. Most people forgot about what happened, but rumors of the massacre were quietly passed down from one generation to the next."

That night, the teens around their campfire in Independence Grove had no reason to disbelieve Katrina's story. The evidence was all around them. Despite the insistence of the local police, and the best efforts of the Lake County Forest Preserve to erase its memory, some kind of institution had been there. For over two decades their friends had gone into those woods and brought back stories of all the artifacts they recovered from what must have been the ruins of the girl's school upon which the story was based.

In fact, the iron gate at the bend in River Road north of Libertyville never led to a girl's school, but the property beyond the gate did serve as a summer camp for boys and girls over a period of sixty years. The real mystery is why the village of Libertyville, which has combated trespassing at the location for years and has spent countless hours denying the rumors of a child massacre, has never made any effort to explain the history behind the property that was formerly known as the "Doddridge Farm." Since its original incarnation as a summer home for children, it passed through many owners and served many purposes before the Lake County Forest Preserve ultimately purchased it and tore down the camp buildings. From the time when the story of "Devil's Gate," or simply "The Gate," began to be noticed by chroniclers of the area's ghostlore, Scott Markus and I have been the only authors to do any significant research on the location. I first began to delve into the "The Gate" in 2002 and made it the focus of the third issue of the *Legends and Lore of Illinois* in March 2007.[1] Since that time, I have had the pleasure of speaking with several men who attended the camp, tracked down dozens of newspaper articles, and am reasonably certain I can construct a reliable, accurate account of the history of the Doddridge Farm and "Devil's Gate."

The story of the Doddridge Farm began in 1925. On January 18, Katharine Doddridge Kreigh Budd, wife of Britton I. Budd, passed away. Britton Budd was the president of the Chicago Rapid Transit Company and the North Shore railroad. Katharine was a philanthropist and had desired for years to open a religious refuge for children. When she died, her husband endeavored to make that aspiration a reality. He chose a picturesque property along the Des Plaines River and set to work. Construction on the Katharine K. Budd Memorial Home for Children began in the spring of 1926 and opening day was set for June 25 of that year. The camp was originally designed to accommodate 150 children in ten separate cottages, but five additional cottages had to be built by the time it opened. A swimming pool, chapel, and home for the Sisters of St. Mary of the western province of the Protestant Episcopal Church, who were entrusted to oversee the camp, were to come later. The Reverend Sheldon M. Griswold, suffragan bishop of Chicago, dedicated the children's memorial home on June 27, 1926.[2] The summer camp was only open for five short years until, in 1931, its board of trustees decided it would better serve the public as an emergency relief home for destitute children and their families. According to the *Daily Tribune*, Mrs. Helen Nixon, former assistant superintendent for a home for crippled children in New York, was hired to run the facility.[3]

In 1936, the Episcopal diocese of Chicago leased the Doddridge Farm, along with its summer camp, to the Boy Scouts of America for a period of two years. After that time expired, the organization had the option of renewing the lease for ten years. We do not have a record of what the property looked like during the 1930s, but the *Daily Tribune* described it as, "a 100 acre tract along the Des Plaines River, 60 acres of which are wooded, with 18 buildings equipped with running water and all modern sanitary facilities, capable of accommodating 200 boys. Safe drinking water is obtained from an artesian well 1,200 feet deep which also supplies the swimming pool."[4] The Boy Scouts used the land rent free for four years, when the Episcopal diocese of Chicago was forced to transfer the property to the Catholic archdiocese of Chicago because of financial difficulties. The year was 1940, when the Second World War raged overseas and the Great Depression still plagued the United States. Almost immediately, the archdiocese made plans to open its doors to refugee children from all over war torn Europe, but primarily Great Britain. A year later, the camp took in needy girls aged 8 to 14. A group of volunteers, organized by the Catholic women's order Ladies of the Grail, made sure that everything ran smoothly. The girls were chosen by both Catholic priests and Chicago welfare agencies, and had to pass dental and medical exams in order to qualify for camp life.[5]

While life at the camp was enjoyable and mostly without incident, there was a brief scare in 1943 that almost turned the legend of "Devil's Gate" into a reality. On September 13, 1943, Sheriff's deputies arrested a watchman at the Catholic Youth camp, along with a male companion, as they drove in the early morning hours northeast of Libertyville. The watchman was carrying a flashlight and a loaded revolver. Deputies took the two men to the Lake County jail, but they both escaped by climbing through a hole in the ceiling. Neither was heard from again, and if the police knew what the men were doing near the girl's camp with a loaded weapon, they did not inform the press.[6]

In 1955, the archdiocese changed the focus of the camp at Doddridge Farm from girls to boys and called it St. Francis Boys Camp. Members of the Franciscan Order took over administration of the facility. According to a 1961 St. Francis guidebook, two priests oversaw the entire

"Devils Gate," Libertyville.

camp and several seminarians, who served as counselors and program supervisors, assisted them. The guidebook described St. Francis Boys Camp as, "Approximately 20 buildings of various sizes and shapes, with screened windows and doors providing excellent living quarters for fun and rest... of these buildings five are used for the living quarters for the campers. Included... are the camp chapel, a spacious dining hall and kitchen, a well-equipped infirmary, a large assembly hall with a stage, a craft shop and the main office building. For swimming, there is the beautiful enclosed swimming pool measuring 30 feet by 75 feet."[7]

Danny Kuczmierczyk attended St. Francis Boys Camp from 1962 to 1965. Having read the *Legends and Lore of Illinois* issue on "Devil's Gate," he wanted to set the record straight about what day-to-day life was like at the summer camp. The following is an excerpt of his remarks.

"I went to Camp Saint Francis in 1962, 1963, 1964, and 1965. It was run by the Franciscans friars who were based in West Chicago. There were five cabins: Grecio (kids 8-9), Sienna (10-11), Padua (12-13), Assisi (older kids), and Capistrano (counselors-in-training). These guys were of the title 'brothers' and the fathers, usually two, kept watch on the cabins. The camp periods were based on two week stints, which started in mid June and ended in mid August. It [lasted] nine weeks.

"There were miscellaneous out buildings; arts and crafts, nature building, auditorium, the resident doctor, the giant mess hall, swimming pool, locker room, and church. There were a lot of activities; arts and crafts (I almost cut my finger off carving a totem pole), archery/rifle range (BB guns), how to identify flora and fauna, and swimming in the big blue pool (this is where I learned). There were lots of sports like soccer and baseball. We also had field events like track and high jump cross country racing. We would play the Serbian kids in baseball games (they were from the Serbian camp that was on the other side of the river).

"And we could go on hikes unsupervised (older kids). This is how we found 'the mansion.' They used to have big parties there in the summer but we were not allowed to go. We would sneak over there. We also participated in President Kennedy's 50 mile walk. Since this was a Catholic camp it was mandatory to go to church on Sundays. There was no getting out of this. There was the movie night and a biweekly talent show (these all took place in the old auditorium), and the nightly campouts (weather permitting). An Indian tribe would come down river in canoes and put on a little show every two weeks. And there was a Saturday night bazaar. Games of skill and prizes. There was also the weekly dining alfresco and marshmallow roasts. There were about 30 kids to a cabin and we all got up the same time in the morning. There was the 9:00pm curfew. The older kids could stay up late.

"Now some spooky stuff. There used to be tales of a guy who lived in the woods and carried an axe. You know the rest. We never heard about the 'school murders,' but the guy who lived in the woods would hack up the campers (ha ha). There were a lot of trails that went through the woods and we were warned not to go at night, even with flashlights. Most of the kids were from Chicago and Sundays were parents visiting day. That's when the big whoppers were told and we would watch our parents gasp. It was fun back then."[8]

A heavy cloud was cast over the camp as it got ready to open for the 1961 summer season. Early that May, a two-year-old boy from the neighboring farm drowned in the river adjacent to St. Francis. "The boy, son of Mr. and Mrs. Paul Bottorff," the *Daily Tribune* reported, "was playing with a sister, Heather, 5, on the grounds of the adjacent St. Francis Home for Boys, a summer camp not yet in use." The girl left her brother alone to run home and ask if they could have a picnic in the woods. When she returned, her brother was gone. The boy's parents formed a search party, but they did not look near the Des Plaines River since they did not believe he could have wandered that far on account of a physical disability. According to the *Tribune*, "in late afternoon, the family dog ran up from the direction of the river, a half mile distant." Searchers followed the dog to the boy's body, which was floating in the murky water.[9]

At some point in the late 1980s or early 1990s, the Catholic arch-diocese sold the Doddridge Farm to the Lake County Forest Preserve. The Forest Preserve quickly made plans to tear down the old camp and reclaim the area as a nature preserve. The 100-acre site was absorbed into over 1,000 acres of land that became known as Independence Grove. Independence Grove was Libertyville's original name, before it was changed in 1837. A former gravel pit formed the centerpiece of the park. It was converted into a lake and christened Independence Lake. The Forest Preserve also laid down a number of trails, one of which winds its way through the former site of Camp St. Francis.[10] While all of the buildings were knocked down and the pool filled in with dirt and debris, the impressive iron gate that led to the camp remains as it always has, at the sharp bend in River Road.

It wasn't long before stories about "Devil's Gate" began to surface. All it took was a new generation to come of age, a generation that had been told to stay out of the woods and away from the ruins of the sum-mer camp. Some adults, it seems, never learn their lesson: when some-thing is forbidden and hushed-up, it becomes mysterious and taboo. Many things should be forbidden, obviously, but not knowledge about something as mundane as a former summer camp. The former Dod-dridge Farm quickly became a focus of intense curiosity among local

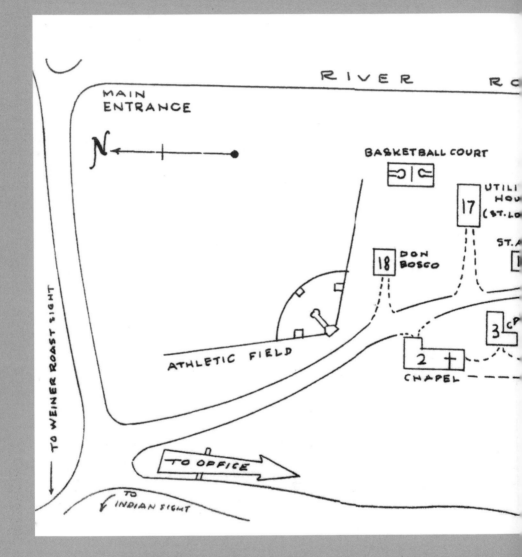

RIVER   R...

MAIN ENTRANCE

N ←———

BASKETBALL COURT

17   UTILI HOU (ST. LO

ST. A

18 DON BOSCO

3 CP

2 ✝

CHAPEL

ATHLETIC FIELD

TO WEINER ROAST SIGHT

TO OFFICE

TO INDIAN SIGHT

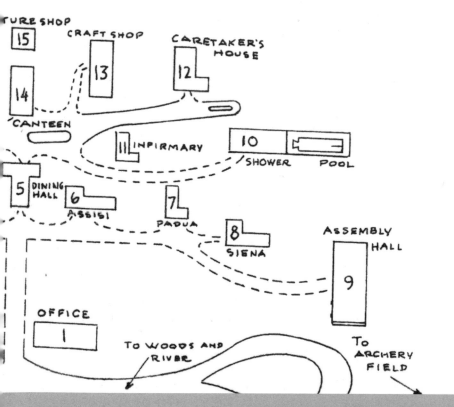

A map of St. Francis Boys Camp, c. 1961.

teens who were ignorant of its history. Why did that institution close? What was it? What was it called? Since nothing but denials and vague warnings answered their questions, they began to make up stories to fill in the blanks. In the words of Ursula Bielski, "Though misled for years, local teenagers have gradually pieced the story together, and it is to prove to themselves the truth of the tale that they have, under cover of darkness, repeatedly ventured into Independence Grove. What do they expect to find?"[11] Nothing, according to the official story of the Forest Preserve and the local police, who have fanned the flames of curiosity with their denials. To keep people from wandering off the trail into the woods, the Forest Preserve recently put up a sign proclaiming the area "ecologically sensitive."

It is difficult to trace when the legend of the child murders first began. As Mr. Kuczmierczyk explained, stories of an ax murderer in the woods circulated St. Francis Boys Camp in the early 1960s. Victoria Pusch, who graduated from Mundelein High School in 1993, told the Chicago *Sun-Times* she had heard the legend of "Devil's Gate" as a freshman, which would have been in 1989 or 1990, right around the time the Forest Preserve bought the Doddridge Farm. In 1999, police arrested five teenagers from Vernon Hills whose foray into the woods at night happened to coincide with the release of the popular film *Blair Witch Project* (1999). That movie followed a fictional group of documentary filmmakers as they investigated a legend in the forest around Burkittsville, Maryland. Two of the teens arrested in Independence Grove claimed that during a previous excursion to the site in 1995, they "saw footprints and paw prints that mysteriously stopped and reappeared," as well as "rusty old lockers." Police handed fines to the group for trespassing, but one of the teens, a young woman named Kiana, said their trip "was worth the $75."[12]

In *Voices from the Chicago Grave*, a man named Sean Ellis Dotson told Scott Markus about an encounter he had in the woods in 2003. Sean and a friend had wandered up the trail after midnight and heard a spine-tingling sound. "Very faint, very distant, yet most assuredly voices... I realized they were the voices of children," he said. Thinking the voices came from fellow trespassers just outside of his visual range, he was even more unnerved when the harmless chatter turned to screams. "I felt sure no human being could emit the horrible cry that pierced my ears." Sean and his friend ran back to their car as quickly as their legs could carry them.[13] Scott Markus reported that other people have heard the disembodied screams, but I have explored every nook and cranny of those woods at least half a dozen times during daylight hours and have never heard anything of the sort. Of course, my own experiences (or lack thereof) do not discount those strange reports, but the lack of proof for the murder story certainly calls them into question.

While many have blurred the line between fact and fiction when it comes to the secrets hidden in Independence Grove, the fact remains that an institution called St. Francis did exist in those woods. The evidence is abundant, but it is slowly being carried off as souvenirs by visitors or has been marked by the Lake County Forest Preserve for destruction. The old cement basketball court remains nestled in the tall prairie grass, and two ropes dangle from the branch of a tree, waiting for a time when they will once again hold the wooden seat of a child's swing. Standing alone in that field, you almost *can* hear the laughter of children, like a vestigial memory drawn from a long-forgotten place in your subconscious. The story of the homicidal maniac and the severed heads of schoolgirls may not be true, but the human imagination is powerful. It can convince us that something terrible happened beyond that Gothic iron gate, and that—sometimes in the dead of night—we can still hear the screams.

Chapter Endnotes

[1] See: Michael Kleen, *Legends and Lore of Illinois* 1 (March 2007): 1-6.

[2] *Daily Tribune* (Chicago) 19 January 1925; *Daily Tribune* (Chicago) 3 March 1926; *Daily Tribune* (Chicago) 28 June 1926.

[3] *Daily Tribune* (Chicago) 1 February 1931.

[4] *Daily Tribune* (Chicago) 23 August 1936.

[5] *Daily Tribune* (Chicago) 4 January 1940; *Daily Tribune* (Chicago) 7 July 1940; *Daily Tribune* (Chicago) 20 July 1941.

[6] *Daily Tribune* (Chicago) 13 September 1943.

[7] Franciscan Friars, National Catholic Camping Association, *St. Francis Boys Camp* (Libertyville: privately printed, 1961), 2.

[8] Danny Kuczmierczyk, letter to the editor, *Legends and Lore of Illinois* 2 (October 2008): 2. Note: Mr. Kuczmierczyk's remarks have been edited for minor grammatical and stylistic considerations.

[9] *Daily Tribune* (Chicago) 12 May 1961.

[10] *Chicago Tribune* (Chicago) 22 August 1995.

[11] Ursula Bielski, *More Chicago Haunts: Scenes from Myth and Memory* (Chicago: Lake Claremont Press, 2000), 53.

[12] *Sun-Times* (Chicago) 4 August 1999.

[13] Scott Markus, *Voices from the Chicago Grave: They're Calling. Will You Answer?* (Holt: Thunder Bay Press, 2008), 7-9.

The Lindbergh Schoolhouse along Shoe Factory Road

For many years, a unique stone building sat nestled between woods and farm fields along a quiet rural road in the far northwest corner of Cook County. One day, the family who rented the building—an old schoolhouse that had been converted into a residence—moved out. Then the bulldozers came. Pavement, manicured lawns, McMansions, and "water retention areas" slowly replaced fields and streams a few miles down from the building along Shoe Factory Road. Suburban families moved into this new subdivision. Traffic increased along the road, which was the only access to the outside world for its residents. Occasionally, their children passed the strange looking house—the only one of its kind they had ever seen—on their way to and from errands or on trips to explore the area around their new home.

"What was that place?" they wondered. Why was it abandoned? Had a gruesome crime occurred there? Some of the kids began to break in and explore the building, unaware that local residents had already begun a campaign to save the old schoolhouse and one of the last remaining links to a fast-vanishing rural past.

This is the story of the Charles A. Lindbergh school—a story that begins in 1929 and ends with a decade long battle for its preservation, rumors of ghosts and murders, and its ultimate demolition to make way for yet another subdivision at the height of the nation's housing bubble. It was a classic struggle between tradition and modernity, character and sameness, all swirling around youthful transgressions and an attempt by local teens to alleviate boredom through destructive storytelling. For one brief ten-year period, historians and lawyers, librarians and developers, village board members and their children found themselves drawn together over a simple schoolhouse. While it did not attract nearly as much attention as the Lindbergh School, an abandoned farm just down the road also served as a place of curiosity for area youth. Both locations spawned rumors of murders and ghosts.

It all began in 1929. At that time, farmhouses and tiny villages occupied the land west of the Des Plaines River. The village of Des Plaines had incorporated as a city only a few years earlier, and the massive tarmac of the O'Hare Airport hadn't yet been envisioned. Out in Hanover

Township, a few miles east of the Fox River, country roads meandered through the cornfields. When they weren't helping on the farm, local children attended class in a one-room schoolhouse. Unfortunately, a fire happened to burn down their old schoolhouse, which was called Helberg and had been there since 1890, so the farming community raised money and built a new one made of stone. It was designed in a Spanish Colonial Revival style—one of the few of its kind—and its cobblestone walls were assembled separately and then raised into place on its wooden frame. Red tile or asphalt covered its roof. In 1929, aviation was a new and exciting pursuit. Just two years earlier, Charles A. Lindbergh had been the first man to fly nonstop from New York to Paris, France, making him a national hero and winning him international fame. The farmers and craftsmen of Hanover Township, therefore, decided to name their new schoolhouse after Charles Lindbergh in honor of his achievements. Construction on the building was completed shortly after classes began there on September 5, 1929.[1]

The school hosted first through eighth grades and employed one full time teacher, Miss Anne Fox, as well as a traveling music instructor named Lauris Moseley. Both students and educator worked to maintain their school. "You had to help the teacher keep the school clean, and the boys would fire the furnace," Florence Jones, a longtime area resident who attended the Lindbergh School as a young girl, reminisced to the *Daily Herald*. "We didn't have janitors in those days."[2] She also spoke highly of her teacher, Miss Fox. "Our teacher was someone you could be proud of," she told Mick Zawislak of the Elgin *Courier-News*. "I always thought to myself, 'I want to dress like Miss Fox when I grow up.' She was always so prim and neat."[3]

Mrs. Jones frequently appeared in newspaper articles to talk about her experiences at the school, but many of Hanover Township's senior citizens were educated there and shared their stories. "We thought that school was so big back then, when now it's so small," Marian Wilkie, who attended the Lindbergh School beginning in 1932, told the *Chicago Tribune*. She recalled ice skating on the pond behind the school during the wintertime.[4] Marge Brettschneider, a member of the last graduating class in 1948, agreed that it was a wonderful place in which to grow up. She fondly remembered Miss Fox's grilled cheese sandwiches, which she served once a week from her waffle iron. Marge's class also went on nature walks and raced sailboats in the pond.[5]

During the 1940s, the system of rural schoolhouses in Illinois was formally abolished, because, thanks to bussing and other transportation, most residents by that time had access to modern school facilities. In 1948, township officials consolidated the area around the Lindbergh School into Elgin Area Unit District 46. Since the Lindbergh School, unlike other one-room schools, was constructed from materials more substantial than wood, someone bought it and converted it into a resi-

Former Lindbergh School
about a month before
it was demolished.

dence, which he or she rented to other families.[6] Walls, plumbing, and modern appliances were added to the interior. I have not been able to determine who purchased the property, but it was rented out for a number of decades. According to Susan S. Benjamin of Historic Certification Consultants, its occupants paid rent directly to the school district.[7]

The old Lindbergh School served as a home for several decades until the last tenants left sometime during the 1990s. *Tribune* staff writer Carri Karuhn reported that newspapers from 1994 were "strewn about" when she visited the building in 1998.[8] In 1996, local historian and writer John Russell Ghrist passed the newly abandoned building and became instantly enamored with it. That October, he joined Roy Miller, whose father was one of the original superintendents of the school, in writing about its plight. He tracked down its owner and inquired about his plans for the building. As it turned out, the owner had recently purchased 400 acres adjacent to the property and made plans to sell the whole package to a land developer. Mr. Ghrist quickly began a letter writing campaign to lobby for the preservation of the old schoolhouse. By the end of the year, however, vandals had also taken an interest. They broke windows and kicked holes in the drywall. Ghrist was furious. "Maybe some of these idiots just happened to pass by this grand structure and thought it was fair game to employ their trade of wrecking something that not only does not belong to them but to fragment an institution that many people were hoping to save," he wrote in a passionate editorial in the *Courier-News*.[9]

By the summer of 1998, an investment group called Shoe Factory, LLC., in partnership with Terrestris Development firm of Oak Brook, had bought the land and made plans to build subdivisions consisting of 1,400 homes alongside condos and a commercial project. They also planned to donate 20 acres of the property to Northern Illinois University.[10] Meanwhile, John Russell Ghrist's campaign gained steam. Adding fuel to his argument that the school should be preserved, an archeological survey of the property in August turned up pottery shards 600 to 1,400 years old, as well as remains of a pioneer dairy farm.[11] Relief came quickly on the heels of that discovery. Near the end of August, Hoffman Estates village president Michael J. O'Malley convinced the Terrestris Development firm to preserve the remains of the Lindbergh School. Several unions associated with the Cook County Building and Construction Trades Council agreed to donate time and manpower to restore the building. "Most of the towns around here are not real old, so it is nice to reach back into the past and preserve what's left," President O'Malley told the *Tribune*.[12]

But preserving the building proved to be harder than it seemed. People began to dump their trash on the property and vandals quickly reversed any progress made on repairs to the doors and windows. To make matters worse, no one came forward who was willing to take on the tremendous financial burden of either moving the building or bringing it up to code. Michael O'Malley died in September 2000, depriving the preservationists of their most powerful ally. In 2002, Dennis Cortesi, president of Terrestris Development firm, publically stated that his company remained interested in donating the former schoolhouse to Hoffman Estates, but that they "realize it is almost impossible to bring the building up to date, and it will cost lots of money to renovate it."[13] Eleven months later, the company petitioned the Hoffman Estates Planning, Building, and Zoning Committee to allow them to demolish the building. John Russell Ghrist, alongside a number of former Lindbergh students and other concerned area residents, showed up at the meeting to protest. "My God, how many homes can they build?" he asked *Tribune* reporter Tom McCann. "One by one, every part of the old way of life here is being bulldozed. We have to make a stand."[14]

"In... three years no one stepped forward willing to take over the expense of rehabbing the building," a consultant for Shoe Factory Road, LLC., replied.[15]

At their November meeting, the village board granted a reprieve in which Ghrist and his allies were given ninety days to come up with a way to save the former Lindbergh School. A report on the property completed by the village estimated the restoration cost could have been as high as $500,000 to $1 million because of the presence of asbestos, a lack of sprinklers, and limited access to parking among a litany of other problems.[16] Nevertheless, several individuals stepped forward with their own plans. The village board collected each proposal—including a wine bistro, church, and community center—and chose one by Kevin and Laura Clerkin to renovate and live in the building. But nearly three years passed and nothing happened. Finally, in the fall of 2005, the Clerkins abandoned their plans when the company for which they mutually worked laid them off and they accepted a new job out of state. The development company wasn't interested in giving them the building anyway, the Clerkins claimed. "They dragged their feet, hoping we would go away, and in the end that's what happened," Laura told the *Daily Herald*. By that time, the developers openly pushed for demolition of the former school and denied that it had any historical value.[17] In the spring of 2006, the Hoffman Estates Planning, Building and Zoning Committee again requested plans to save the Lindbergh School.

At a meeting in March, the board voted six to one to raise funds to move the building across the street. They estimated the move would cost at least $350,000. Around that same time, Terrestris Development sold the property to Ryland Homes. Ryland offered to donate $100,000 to the village for the former schoolhouse's preservation, but the village board decided the money would be better spent somewhere else. By the spring of 2007, they were negotiating a demolition contract. Not all the members of the board were in favor of demolition, but they felt their hands were tied by the amount of money involved. At a board meeting in May, Trustee Cary Collins moved to have the village of Hoffman Estates pay the million dollar tab, but no one was willing to second the motion. Instead, the board voted to have the former Lindbergh schoolhouse bulldozed. "History doesn't seem to be important to people," Pat Barch, a local historian, responded. "I'm very sad about all that happened."[18]

Village officials toured the building for the final time in June 2007, but the hopes of preservationists were raised when, that same month, a doctor named Bob Tiballi came forward and offered to donate $100,000. The board voted 4 to 3 to grant a 60-day reprieve while Dr. Tiballi prepared his proposal. In August, the board voted to reject the money offered by Ryland Homes and formally removed itself from any plans to save the schoolhouse.[19] That did not prevent Dr. Tiballi from brokering his own deal with the landowners, but he evidently abandoned his plan. Bulldozers tore through the former Lindbergh School sometime in late August or early September, shortly after I devoted an issue of the *Legends and Lore of Illinois* to the location.[20]

I was a freshman in high school when John Russell Ghrist first drove past the Lindbergh School. Shortly over a year later, the family of a friend of mine moved to the first subdivision built along Shoe Factory Road, and my friend also became curious about the erstwhile schoolhouse. Like most newly-arrived residents, he was not aware of what it was or who owned it. The area was still quiet then, and very few cars passed up and down Shoe Factory Road. There were no stores, libraries, parks, or restaurants around for miles. The abandoned shell of the Lindbergh School was the only interesting landmark. With its unusual architecture and its tendency to appear suddenly after miles of fields and trees, it was a beacon for the curious. Unfortunately, some of those visitors had less than noble intentions, but all wondered about the building and its origins. That's when the stories began to appear.

The Shadowlands Haunted Places Index, an often copied digital repository of rumored hauntings, was the first website to publicize the ghost stories of Shoe Factory Road. The old Lindbergh School and the nearby abandoned farm were often included in the same entry, and they have been on the website since at least 2002. Entries in the Index are written based on user-generated content, so one or more persons who knew of the schoolhouse, barn, and silo wrote into the website to inform its editors of the following (punctuation has been added):

"…If you go a lot father [*sic*] you can then see a barn on the right side and it is said that seventeen years ago that a man escaped from the psycho ward and was staying in the barn, but when the owners of the house found out and tried to get rid of him he killed the family and they were found hanging in the barn. You can see lights on in the barn sometimes. Little more down you see an abandoned house on the left [Lindbergh] where a child killed his parents five years ago because they treated him like a child. If you drive pass [*sic*] the house there are roses on the street sometimes and you can see a child playing on the steps with a knife."[21]

The legend of the killer ghost child may have originated with the wallpaper in one room of the former schoolhouse. The wallpaper featured various colorful balloons and cartoon animals. In the minds of trespassers, that alone would have been enough evidence to confirm the veracity of the story, which explained why a family with a young child would have abruptly abandoned their home. More difficult to explain, however, was the legend associated with the nearby dilapidated farm. One version of the legend, according to a contributor to the Shadowlands Haunted Places Index, went like this:

"The legend is a man went crazy because he thought his wife was cheating on him, so he murdered her and his kids. He killed himself as well. There is also a five-point star located about 20 yards from where he buried his family. The star has a dead tree at each point of the star. Apparently you can still hear noises and see something moving around in the house late at night. Even if it is 80 degrees outside you can feel a bitter uninviting chill."[22]

There appears to be no explanation behind that story. It is untrue, as far as I am aware, and seems to have originated in the imagination of some area resident. The farm, along with its barn and the rest of its buildings save the concrete silo, was torn down around the same time as the old Lindbergh School.

Only a handful of newspaper articles mentioned the rumors of ghosts. In October 2005, the Elgin *Courier-News* published an article titled "Schoolhouse not haunted but not fixed yet, either," right around the time Laura and Kevin Clerkin gave up their plans to turn the building into a residence. The article quoted from the Haunted Places Index, but flatly denied the stories. "It turns out... that the old schoolhouse actually has become a haunt for vandals, who break into it consistently to see what amounts to graffiti," reporter Janelle Walker wrote.[23] Given the remoteness of the location, even with subdivisions newly surrounding it, it is doubtful that very many people who read the Haunted Places Index actually went there. But a few did, as evidenced by the videos of excursions to the building posted on websites such as YouTube.com.

Rachel Brooks has been the only author other than myself to write about the legends of Shoe Factory Road's abandoned sites. In *Chicago Ghosts*, she shared her own personal encounter with the silo on the derelict farm. The story behind it, according to her, was that a man had

The "haunted" silo, with suburban
sprawl in the background.
Photo by the author.

been hanged inside. "As a curious teen," she wrote, "friends and I often drove to the silo with the intention of looking inside to get a glimpse of the macabre blood-stained interior... We were always too chicken, though, and rarely ventured far from the car."[24]

As of today, both the former Lindbergh School and the nearby farm have joined the growing list of landmarks plowed over to make room for suburban sprawl, making land developers the ultimate vandals. Ghost stories or no ghost stories, the Lindbergh School was an important part of Hanover Township's past and it will be missed by many. Florence Jones, who saw her childhood memories disappear under the tread of bulldozers, said it best: "People say they're moving here for the country, and what they're doing is destroying the country."[25]

Chapter Endnotes

[1]Susan S. Benjamin, *Historic and Architectural Assessment: Charles A. Lindbergh School* (Chicago: Historic Certification Consultants, 1998), 3.
[2]*Daily Herald* (Arlington Heights) 9 July 1998.
[3]*Courier-News* (Elgin) 9 August 1998.
[4]*Chicago Tribune* (Chicago) 10 November 2002.
[5]*Daily Herald* (Arlington Heights) 10 November 2002.
[6]*Daily Herald* (Arlington Heights) 9 July 1998.
[7]Benjamin, 5.
[8]*Chicago Tribune* (Chicago) 17 July 1998.
[9]*Courier-News* (Elgin) 6 January 1997.
[10]*Daily Herald* (Arlington Heights) 9 July 1998.
[11]*Daily Herald* (Arlington Heights) 1 August 1998.
[12]*Chicago Tribune* (Chicago) 27 August 1998.
[13]*Chicago Tribune* (Chicago) 6 January 2002.
[14]*Chicago Tribune* (Chicago) 10 November 2002.
[15]*Daily Herald* (Arlington Heights) 10 November 2002.
[16]*Chicago Tribune* (Chicago) 18 November 2002; *Daily Herald* (Arlington Heights) 20 November 2002.
[17]*Daily Herald* (Arlington Heights) 3 November 2005.
[18]*Chicago Tribune* (Chicago) 15 March 2006; *Daily Herald* (Arlington Heights) 9 May 2007; *Chicago Tribune* (Chicago) 9 May 2007.
[19]*Daily Herald* (Arlington Heights) 12 June 2007; *Daily Herald* (Arlington Heights) 14 August 2007.
[20]See: Michael Kleen, *Legends and Lore of Illinois* 1 (August 2007): 1-6.
[21]Shadowlands Haunted Places Index, "Haunted Places in Illinois," < http://theshadowlands.net/places/illinois.htm> (26 June 2009).
[22]Ibid.
[23]*Courier-News* (Elgin) 23 October 2005.
[24]Rachel Brooks, *Chicago Ghosts* (Atglen: Schiffer Books, 2008), 115-116.
[25]*Chicago Tribune* (Chicago) 10 November 2002.

Ashmore Estates:
The Myth and the Legend

It was a hot July day in 2008. I stood on a concrete step outside the weathered, brick façade of Ashmore Estates, attempting to attach a small microphone to my shirt collar. Amanda Evans from WCIA Channel 3 News waited patiently for a quote, something that would neatly tie her whole segment together. Nearby, Philip Adrian and Christopher Saint Booth, otherwise known as the Booth Brothers—producers of *Spooked* (2006), *Children of the Grave* (2007), and *The Possessed* (2009)—milled around the lawn in their cowboy boots and Stetson hats. Why was this long-abandoned building so important? the reporter asked me. Why had I felt compelled to devote long hours to researching its history and folklore?

I cleared my throat and fumbled for the right words.

"I think anything that doesn't have to do with [President] Lincoln around Coles County—'cause it's a big thing around here—any kind of other history is good for people to know about," I stuttered.

The segment was broadcast on the evening news all over central Illinois.

It wasn't everyday that two producers from Los Angeles found themselves in rural Coles County, especially not to shoot a television program for the Sci-Fi Channel. In this case, it was a sequel to their widely acclaimed *Children of the Grave*, which would focus on a local legend—*a building*—that has risen from virtual obscurity to become a center of attention for fans of the paranormal around the United States and, more recently, the world.

It began with humble origins. For twenty years Ashmore Estates was a minor curiosity and a magnet for strange stories of every sort, especially for students at nearby Eastern Illinois University in Charleston. A generation of trespassers and thrill seekers risked injury and arrest to explore the cavernous interior of this building, or in the expressive words of journalist David Thill, "for years, teenagers and college students alike have journeyed to this decrepit tower of terror."[1] It has stood abandoned outside the village of Ashmore since 1987, every subsequent year falling prey to vandalism and neglect, until its recent rehabilitation as a haunted attraction. Since its reopening in 2006, Ashmore Estates has attracted national attention for its alleged hauntings, but few are aware of the real history behind the legend.

Ashmore Estates, along with the adjacent farmland, was originally called the Coles County Poor Farm. From 1857 until 1869, the county poor farm resided in Charleston Township near the small town of Loxa, but in 1870, the county purchased 260 acres from A. N. Graham in Section 35 of Ashmore Township for a new farm. "The brick for the building was made and burned on the county farm just across the railroad on the south side," Ben R. Maxwell, a contractor from Charleston who worked on the project as a young man, told the *Daily Courier*.[2]

The small timber and brick building, constructed by H. B. Truman, was the first to sit on that lot, and the initial superintendent of the county farm was Oliver D. Hawkins, who immigrated to Coles County from Kentucky in 1841. He quickly rose to become a prominent member of the Ashmore community, and was the chairman of the Finance Committee at the time Coles County bought the land near Ashmore for use as a poor farm. He served as superintendent of the farm for three years. This almshouse once sheltered between thirty and forty people, among them a cousin of General Winfield Scott, a hero of the Mexican War, but its population gradually trickled away. According to Coles County census data, the farm housed 41 residents in 1870 (including twelve under the age of ten), 35 in 1880, 23 in 1900, and 18 in 1910.

Medical care was sparse and many people died inside the building. In 1907, the salary of the attending physician was only sixty dollars a year.[3] The county maintained a small cemetery somewhere north of the grounds, as well as another that still exists south of Route 16 and contains the graves of between sixty to one hundred persons.[4] According to local mortuary records, in February of 1880, a seven-year-old girl named Elva L. Skinner burned to death inside the almshouse. In 2004, I published *Tales of Coles County, Illinois*, a collection of historical fiction stories touching on the underbelly of Coles County history. One of the tales took place in the almshouse during the Great Depression, using Elva Skinner as a ghost that tormented the main character. Much to my surprise, some people began to believe that modern day Ashmore Estates is actually haunted by her ghost. In October 2006, the *Coles County Leader* reported, "other spirits identified [in the building] are that of a little girl, Evita [*sic*] Skinner…" One paranormal investigator even claimed to record her voice on tape![5]

After the turn of the century, the Auxiliary Committee of the State Board of Charities condemned the building for its appalling conditions, which included "vermin infected walls," "rough floors," "small windows," and improper ventilation. It was reported that "flies swarmed everywhere" and "were especially noticeable on the poor food prepared for dinner." Additionally, the residents were found to be mostly elderly and unsupervised. The Auxiliary Committee felt so strongly about their

Ashmore Estates, Ashmore, c. 2001.
Photo by the author.

decision that they remarked, "our pride and our humanity should make us determined to remove the disgrace of it from us."[6] In January 1915, the Almshouse Committee, headed up by John Goodyear, Ivory W. Merritt, Jr., E.N. Carter, W.R. Zimmerman, and William Knollenberg, received bids for the construction of a new "fireproof" building at the location.[7]

The building contract for the new almshouse was first awarded to S.C. Sailor of Oak Wood, Illinois, but he backed out of the project in late February 1916. The contract was then granted to J.W. Montgomery in March of 1916 for $20,389, and the cornerstone was ceremoniously laid on May 17, 1916. While builders set the cornerstone in place, "the spectators spent considerable time in visiting the inmates of the home and looking around the big farm."[8] According to the Charleston *Daily Courier*, the metal box in the cornerstone contained a Bible, a book of rules of the County Board, the minutes of the supervisor's meeting that authorized the construction of a new almshouse, and copies of three local newspapers.[9] The architect who designed the building was L.F.W. Stuebe, and it was scheduled to be completed by September 1st of that same year.

Life on the new farm was markedly better than on the old. A full time caretaker and his family took turns living in the almshouse and in a white farmhouse that formerly sat on the property. In 2006, I had the pleasure of speaking to Nancy Swinford, who was the daughter of Leo Roy and Lura Andrews, the supervisors of the farm after the Second World War. Nancy lived at the home for eight years, from around 1947 to 1954, starting at the age of eight or nine.

Leo Roy "Bill" Andrews was the superintendent of the farm during that period, and his wife Lura was known as the matron. Bill was in charge of managing the farm itself, while Lura supervised life inside the building, including laundry detail and meal preparation for her family and the residents. "The county furnished all the food," Nancy recollected. A breadbox sat at the end of the driveway, where a bread man would deliver twice a week. He occasionally left sweet rolls. The residents churned their own butter. Maple trees filled the poor farm yard, and a hedge ran around the outside of the lawn and down the driveway. Cattle stayed in a large barn located south of the main building, which is still in existence today. A smoke-house, a chicken house, and a two-car garage also sat on the land. The superintendent's house, which is now located in the town of Ashmore, was heated by a basin burner in the winter.

The residents of the farm were mostly poor and indigent. They were assigned to live there by the county and some had spent time in jail. "The people that lived there were people who had no homes and no families," Nancy said. "It was before all your fancy nursing homes. They were all ages; a lot more men than there were women." On average, there would be around eight women and fifteen men residing there at any given time. Most of them stayed at the farm for the duration of their lives and were expected to work. "We had some who would help in the kitchen," Nancy explained. "They would help with the cooking. Some helped with the dishes. They had responsibilities. They milked cows. They butchered all their own meat. Those that were able... daddy gave them a job. They had to help earn their piece."

Each man and woman living on the farm had his or her own distinctive personality and eccentricities. One resident that Nancy recalled in particular was named Red Carmen, known as "Red" because of his red hair. She remembered that he always wore a fedora hat. Another man, known as "Tiny" despite his large size, used to spend hours sitting on the stone porch steps. Nancy reminisced in particular about two women who shared a room. One called the other "grandma." "She was very small," Nancy explained. "She passed away there. I remember seeing my mother close her eyes." The residents were ordinarily friendly, although Nancy explained that "once in a while there were people who were a little scary."[10]

Eventually, poor farms fell out of use as Illinois counties no longer wanted to expend the funds to keep them maintained. Many of them were simply sold off to private farmers, but others were privatized as care facilities. Coles County retained the farmland around the property, but sold the almshouse to Ashmore Estates, Inc. in February 1959. That corporation opened the building as a private psychiatric hospital, but it suffered from financial difficulties from the very beginning. In October 1964, the psychiatric hospital closed down because of "terrible debt," as building supervisor Neva Brown explained in a newspaper article written by Allan Keith for the *Courier-News*. The institution reopened in 1965, and changed its focus from a private facility to one that accepted patients from state mental institutions. By 1968, the shelter care facility housed forty-nine residents, including ten afflicted with epilepsy. According to Keith, "patients at the home have available a full-time recreational program, including games and arts and crafts. Protestant church services are conducted on Sundays and Friday nights."[11] Dr. Wayne T. Neal, a Mattoon resident, was head of the corporation, chief administrator, and also provided all medical services for the patients.

Paul Swinford (no relation to Mary Swinford) and Galen Martinie purchased the institution in July 1976. The two originally envisioned building a brand new, one floor residency to house up to one hundred patients, but according to journalist Robert Themer, "the state planning committee refused to approve that plan after considering it for six months."[12] Consequently, Swinford and Martinie invested over two hundred thousand dollars in the construction of a modern addition onto the old building. Construction began in 1977, but was not yet finished when controversy embroiled Ashmore Estates in the summer of 1979.

On May 2 of that year, the Illinois Department of Public Health ordered the institution closed after finding twenty two safety code violations, including fire safety issues, exposed wiring, problems with exit maintenance, and construction debris. According to one representative of the Coles County social services, some areas of the building were "like a ghetto."[13] Acting Public Health Director Byron J. Francis gave Swinford and Martinie ten days to remove the residents, but the two owners filed an affidavit with the Coles County Circuit Court for an injunction to delay or suspend the order. Mr. Swinford argued that they had made considerable progress in fixing the violations. The Illinois Department of Public Health responded by recommending that the Public Aid Department decertify the institution and cease making monthly payments in excess of nineteen thousand dollars for the care of its thirty three public aid recipients.[14]

On May 17, Coles County Circuit Court Judge Joseph Spitz, alongside Paul Swinford, Galen Martinie, James Linder of the Department of Public Health, and a representative of the Attorney General's office, toured the building to see if any progress had been made in fixing the violations. James Linder was satisfied with some of the repairs, but not others. According to Carl Green of the *Times-Courier*, Linder told Judge Spitz, "it's as if somebody waved a wand in here."[15] He was unimpressed, however, with the emergency electrical system, which needed to be manually switched on and failed to light the basement hallway. Six days after the tour, Judge Joseph Spitz granted a one hundred and twenty day reprieve so that the necessary repairs could be completed. Periodic inspections were to be made during that time, with a final licensing inspection by the Department of Public Health upon conclusion of a second judicial hearing.[16]

Once the addition to Ashmore Estates had been completed and the rest of the building brought up to code, the institution's future appeared brighter. On December 12, 1981, Barbara Jean Clark became director of the care facility and expressed optimism about the future. "We have the opportunity to be one of the best facilities of our kind in the area," she remarked in their eight page in-house organ, *The Ashmore Review*.[17] Mark Temples, whose wife, Jane, worked at the facility as an assistant nurse, was managing editor of that publication—nicknamed *The Good Newspaper*—along with co-editor Monte Henson. He recalled that finding clients after 1980 had been difficult, but over time the state referred a satisfactory number to the institution. "It took them awhile to get enough people to justify the... expenditures," he informed me in a candid interview in 2006.

While the residents enjoyed leisure activities, which included their own basketball team that practiced at the Ashmore gymnasium, there were occasional tensions between the upper level management and the service staff. "They first of all weren't paid what they thought they should be paid," Mark explained. "The working conditions were pretty deplorable. Some of these patients could get out of hand... they were taken with fits of rage. I knew of one [employee] personally who got beaten up pretty badly by a patient. One of the things they wanted were guarantees these types of things wouldn't happen." Most of the residents were harmless. Mark remembered two in particular, one girl named Susan Pullman, who had fallen out of a van and consequently suffered from severe head injuries, the other, "a little guy named Kenny Shepherd." Shepherd "was very reticent and very nice," he recalled. "They were just on the edge of not being able to live on their own."[18]

On Christmas Eve, 1981, the residents exchanged presents in the morning and enjoyed a Christmas dinner "with all the trimmings" at noon. They were then allowed to leave and spend the holiday with family or friends, but had to return early the next day on account of a snowstorm warning. Their six-member basketball team, coached by Tim Carter and Tom Dunn, received their own jerseys on December

30th courtesy of a number of charitable contributors such as Jim Hall of Hall Equipment and Max Cooper of Anderson Reality, among others.[19]

Curt Starkey, currently a behavioral health therapist in Charleston, worked as Director of Psychological Services at the institution in conjunction with John Grimes from 1982 to 1983. "During the period I was there the residents were treated pretty well," he told me. However, he explained that some of the residents were "rough," and that Ashmore Estates had taken on a half dozen patents during that period who were "extremely violent." The staff frequently had to obtain doctor's orders to use chemical or physical restraints. In one episode, a woman who Starkey described as "possessed" broke her restraints and physically assaulted him. Despite these conditions, the staff closely followed procedures.[20]

In February 1986, Paul Swinford entered into a limited partnership with a Peoria company known as Convalescent Management Associates, Inc. to help manage the institution's finances. The departments of Public Aid and Public Health dragged their feet over the issuance of proper licenses and certificates for nearly a year, leading Swinford to file for permission to close the facility from the Illinois Health Facility Planning Board. At that time, Ashmore Estates' financial losses exceeded one and a half million dollars.[21] "There wasn't enough patients coming into the system, and there were major repairs needed for the structure itself," Mark Temples explained. "The money that it would have taken to bring them up to code on all this stuff just wasn't there."[22]

Convalescent Management Associates, Inc. terminated their contract with Swinford in March 1987 after the company was forced to dole out funds for the employee payroll, a responsibility they vehemently denied. "The employees were never employees of CMA," a spokesman told the Times-Courier. "They continue to be employees of Ashmore Estates."[23] Mr. Swinford then joined with Residential Alternatives, a Charleston company, who took on the role of "transitional management" while new homes were built for the residents of the facility. Employees of Ashmore Estates were caught in the middle and did not receive pay for two weeks at the end of March, despite receiving a monetary gift from Busey Bank in Urbana, Illinois, the same bank that foreclosed on a loan to Ashmore Estates in early March, an action which contributed to the pay crisis.[24]

By the end of April, all of the residents had been transferred to area homes, and Ashmore Estates closed its doors. According to Dave Fopay of the *Times-Courier,* Paul Swinford, who still owned the building, blamed the closure on "the state's shift on how to care for the mentally retarded," but a longtime resident of the area, Gerald Ferguson, disagreed. "He didn't keep things up the way he was supposed to,"

Ferguson argued. "He said he didn't get the state funds but he didn't meet their regulations."[25]

For the next nineteen years, the building went through multiple tax disputes and perspective owners, all the while falling into neglect and disrepair. As all the former residents, administrators, and staff moved on, vandalism, rumors, and ghost stories moved in.

It would be three years before anyone endeavored to reopen the institution. In 1990, Paul Swinford, in conjunction with a Tennessee company known as Corrections Corporation of America, attempted to turn Ashmore Estates into a mental health facility for teenage boys. Many local residents, who "were concerned about what the facility's patients might do if they escaped," spoke out against the plan.[26] At a public hearing that November, a rural Ashmore resident named April Karrick presented a petition signed by over 240 local residents expressing their opposition.[27] On the night of December 18, the Ashmore Village Board rejected Swinford's request for a zoning permit by a vote of five to zero, effectively dooming the project over concerns related to fire safety, as well as consideration for public opposition.[28] Mr. Swinford unsuccessfully appealed the decision early the next year.

Between 1991 and 1993, over $15,000 in back taxes on the property went unpaid. In June 1994, the county sold the tax debt to a Decatur real estate broker named Dennis Ballinger, who gained the legal right to collect the taxes for the county. Three and a half months later, the Coles County Court awarded Mr. Ballinger the deed to the property after Paul Swinford failed to come forward with any of the tax money, but Mr. Swinford later paid a large portion of the delinquent taxes, and the county refunded Mr. Ballinger for the money he had already paid. The deed to Ashmore Estates reverted to Paul Swinford.[29]

Meanwhile, the structure continued to deteriorate. In early November 1995, a fire destroyed a storage building that sat across the lawn from the front entrance of the main building, where the poor farm superintendent's house once stood.[30] The peach, cinderblock remains of the interior withstood the test of time until the most recent owners removed it to make room for their home.

By the summer of 1996, the Coles County Board, encouraged by Environmental Health Director Dan Stretch, debated over whether or not to condemn the building and expunge it from the public consciousness once and for all. "It does need to be torn down," Stretch told Dave Fopay of the *Times-Courier* more than a year after the controversy. "The cost to rehabilitate it probably wouldn't justify fixing it."[31] Confusion over ownership (Mr. Swinford held the deed but still owed around $9,000 in unpaid taxes) halted the effort.

By that time, aided by a steady rotation of students from outside of the county who were unaware of its history, Ashmore Estates had become a minor legend on the campus of Eastern Illinois University in Charleston. For the Halloween issue of the Verge section of the *Daily Eastern News*, Mike Rice and Matt Fear, the "Men of Adventure," wrote a satirical piece on how to make Ashmore Estates into a "highly illegal" Halloween escapade. "No one is really sure what this building once housed," they wrote. "But there are stories. These tales revolve around pagan rituals and dismembered bodies. We aren't sure if any of them are true or not, but they sure do make for three floors... of unadulterated fun."[32] The two also described "possibly" encountering a severed pig's head in the stairwell, but creative license may have been the origin of that macabre detail.

Two years after the County Board contemplated the destruction of the building, they decided to put it up for auction instead. According to former County Treasurer Bill Grimes, Paul Swinford had been sent tax bills for the previous three years but again failed to pay. Journalist Dave Fopay explained that Swinford, "has told people interested in buying the property that he doesn't own it anymore."[33] That left Coles County with the legal right to sell the property at auction if no one came forward to object. In July, Ashmore Estates, along with the more than two acres of land surrounding it, was added to the annual surplus property auction, back taxes not included.

Bidding began at $2,000, and around forty people showed up to express their intent to purchase the building. At the end of the day, a Sullivan man named Arthur Colclasure paid $12,500 for the property, and announced that he planned to renovate the building and turn it into his home.[34] Mr. Colclasure's battle to rehabilitate the structure carried on for over a year. Like Sisyphus condemned to push a boulder endlessly up the side of a hill, trespassers and vandals countered every step he made towards repairing the damage. "I keep putting [windows] in and they keep breaking them out," he told Dave Fopay in the summer of 1999.[35] His goal at the time was to fully secure the building in time for winter, but to my knowledge that goal was never met.

My first encounter with Ashmore Estates occurred just after Eastern Illinois University's winter break in January 2001. So effective were the vandals at thwarting Colclasure's efforts that it did not appear to me that anyone owned the building or had ever tried to repair it. I had briefly heard of the place from my roommate the previous year, and I went there at the insistence of a friend, although she did not need to do much prodding. From what I recall, the building was just as much a shell then as it is now, although a few worn out pieces of furniture were arranged in one room, guarded by a rubber, severed hand.

In spite of endless dead ends and a sparse pile of inaccurate or incomplete information, I attempted to gather all the available data on the building over the next several years, although my efforts were occasionally exploited. I was surprised to find an article in the November 2004 issue of the *Pulse*, a magazine published by

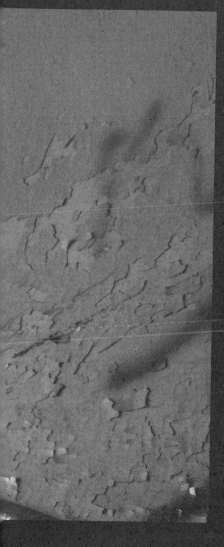

Graffiti adorns the walls
inside Ashmore Estates.

Eastern Illinois University's University Board, where a great deal of my research data was used to bring the truth out—especially that of Ashmore Estates. Additionally, though it didn't ring true to me, there was an article alongside that talked about the author's aborted night at the "asylum."[36]

In June 2006, I devoted an issue of my electronic serial, also named *Legends and Lore of Coles County*, to Ashmore Estates.[37] Not long after I predicted a dismal end to the building in that issue, a man named Scott Kelley, who owned a local computer company and also operated haunted houses during the month of October, contacted me and informed me that he had plans to rent or even purchase the property.

Scott Kelley and his wife, Tanya, first became interested in Ashmore Estates around ten years earlier. Scott, a longtime operator of haunted house attractions including the local haunts at Elsinore Farm and Rockome Gardens, believed the institution would make an excellent haunted house. "A couple of times since then we came close to moving by the building," he told me. "Now nine years later I own it and have brought my dream to life."

The Kelleys purchased the property from Arthur Colclasure in early August and immediately began renovating. According to Scott, "the building was a wreck... it took seven weeks of forty hours a week to clean it out... the windows were mostly broken."[38] To finance the project, the Kelleys offered flashlight tours of the interior for five dollars a person. To discourage trespassers, they erected signs and moved into a trailer on the property. These efforts were not always successful. According to Rob Stroud of the *Times-Courier*, on at least one occasion the Kelleys called the County Sheriff after several young adults snuck into the building at night. On another occasion, a cemetery headstone mysteriously found its way onto the property and then disappeared several days later.[39]

After months of painstaking cleaning and preparation, the haunted house opened its doors from October 13 thru the 31st. From 7pm until 10:30pm, adults paid $12 and children $9 to see what they had always imagined lurking inside Ashmore Estates come to life. The interior had been radically transformed, however. Kelley's graphic artist, Brandon Stevens, removed or obscured all of the potentially offensive graffiti, and large barriers divided the hallways. Participants were led into the building through a side door and past the old boiler room. Once inside, they wound down the darkened hallways, past old nurse's stations and vacant quarters. Rooms where the elderly and destitute once slept, where patients once daydreamed, and where the walls had been covered with "Duffy" in red paint, actors and actresses made up like characters in a 1960s horror movie shrieked at groups of thrilled spectators. The cold and the rain that first Halloween failed to keep the crowd away.

Several "ghost hunting" groups have combed the interior since its reopening in 2006, which has generated some controversy in the community among those who perceive such groups in a negative light. In June 2008, Ursula Bielski and Edward L. Shanahan brought twenty people on an overnight stay at Ashmore Estates as part of a series of events known as "Beyond the Veil." Sean Flanagan was among the participants. "Stepping into the building on the initial tour, I was surprised by the feelings that took over," he told me. "I thought feelings of intimidation and fear would quickly rise. Instead, I realized that the building is just that, a building... I felt calm and at ease. There were a couple of rooms where I felt 'something.' There seemed to be a presence in these couple of rooms that I did not feel elsewhere." After eating dinner with Ursula and Edward, the amateur investigators gathered their equipment.

"Three groups were to enter the building at a time, one per floor," Sean explained. "We were paired up with another couple and two other guys, all on their first investigation. Through the night, we investigated all three floors. There were several points throughout the building where there [were] unexpected spikes on the EMF meter. There was also a point where 'yes and no' questions seemed to get consistent responses or 'answers' on the K2 meter. Lighting up the meter once for yes and twice for no helped us find out that we were dealing with a young girl who wasn't very happy (almost a year later, I do not recall anything more specific). The feelings of calmness and fascination were present for most, if not the entire investigation. There was excitement as well. Excitement in that the energy spikes and responses on the K2 could be those of an energy of someone once living! Upon reviewing my tapes of the various EVP sessions, I may have heard my first EVP. Hearing what could be the voice of a disembodied spirit is quite an incredible feeling."[40]

Janice Tremeear, member of a group called the Southwest Ghost Finders, related her own experiences during a recent investigation of the building. "After equipment had been set up I checked on a camera, recorder and ELF [a type of EMF detector that measures electromagnetic field radiation levels] on the third floor. The ELF and recorder were dead, with new batteries. Five of us were standing still as we switched out equipment and a cardboard barrel behind us was kicked into the wall directly to my right," she told me. "At 5am we were picking up a lot of activity with our K2 meters. There had been intermitted [sic] hits all night long but while most of the team slept, four of us went back to the third floor where someone was playing with us leading, us from room to room."[41]

This activity culminated in the building's inclusion in the Booth Brother's *Children of the Grave 2* (or as it came to be known, *Soul Catcher*). It has also been featured in *American Horrors*, a television special airing in Europe. Tyson Reed, executive producer of the episode in the series featuring Ashmore Estates, was excited to have the opportunity to film there. "I am really happy that the new owners are keeping up with the building and doing their best to prolong its life so all can enjoy and maybe even experience something of their own during a visit," he said. "Basing the documentary on factual history was the goal of the project, and dramatized or not, the things talked about and discussed are more realistic than people may want to believe. We had a number of strange things happen to us throughout the filming of the project. We were followed by police, shunned by townspeople, and even warned of facts we may disclose." Nevertheless, he was determined to have the story told. "Places like Ashmore Estates are very interesting and I think it is important for people to take the time and understand how things use to be, no matter how crude or strange," he explained.[42]

The media attention will undoubtedly place Ashmore Estates at the forefront of haunted attractions in Illinois for years to come.

From an almshouse, to a psychiatric hospital, to a care facility, the institution popularly known as Ashmore Estates has run the gauntlet of public and private healthcare in Illinois. The abandonment and deterioration of the building, and its subsequent use as an instrument of entertainment and paranormal-themed fun, is just the most recent chapter of a long and sordid past. I believe that the residents of Coles County, as well as anyone interested in this fascinating place, would be best served by fully understanding its complex history.

Chapter Endnotes

[1]*Daily Eastern News* (Charleston) 12 March 2004.
[2]*Daily Courier* (Charleston) 24 May 1916.
[3]*Journal Gazette* (Mattoon) 30 March 1907.
[4]*Times-Courier* (Charleston), 20 July 2001.
[5]*Coles County Leader* (Tuscola), 27 October 2006.
[6]*Daily Courier* (Charleston) 12 August 1911.
[7]*Daily Courier* (Charleston) 11 January 1915.
[8]*Daily Courier* (Charleston) 1 March 1916.
[9]*Daily Courier* (Charleston) 18 May 1916.
[10]Nancy Swinford, interview by author, 26 October 2006.
[11]*Courier-News* (Charleston) 17 August 1968.
[12]*Times-Courier* (Charleston) 11 May 1979.
[13]*Times-Courier* (Charleston) 10 May 1979.
[14]*Times-Courier* (Charleston) 11 May 1979.
[15]*Times-Courier* (Charleston) 18 May 1979.
[16]*Times-Courier* (Charleston) 24 May 1979.
[17]*The Ashmore Review* (Ashmore Estates, Ashmore) 30 December 1981.
[18]Mark Temples, interview by author, 12 August 2006.
[19]*The Ashmore Review* (Ashmore Estates, Ashmore) 30 December 1981.
[20]Curt Starkey, interview by author, 31 May 2007.
[21]*Times-Courier* (Charleston) 14 April 1987.

[22]Mark Temples, interview by author, 12 August 2006.
[23]*Times-Courier* (Charleston) 14 April 1987.
[24]*Times-Courier* (Charleston) 17 April 1987.
[25]*Times-Courier* (Charleston) 8 June 1991.
[26]*Times-Courier* (Charleston) 30 June 1994.
[27]*Times-Courier* (Charleston) 18 December 1990.
[28]*Times-Courier* (Charleston) 19 December 1990.
[29]*Times-Courier* (Charleston) 14 October 1994.
[30]*Times-Courier* (Charleston) 2 November 1995.
[31]*Times-Courier* (Charleston, IL) 17 January 1998.
[32]*Daily Eastern News* (Charleston) 31 October 1997.
[33]*Times-Courier* (Charleston) 17 January 1998.
[34]*Times-Courier* (Charleston) 29 July 1998.
[35]*Times-Courier* (Charleston) 3 July 1999.
[36]See: Paulina Andorf, "Ashmore Estates: an Evening at the Abandoned Insane Asylum," *The Pulse Publication* 1, no. 2 (2004): 18-19.
[37]See: Michael Kleen, "Ashmore Estates," *Legends and Lore of Coles County, Illinois* 1, no. 4 (2006).
[38]Scott Kelley, interview by author, 18 May 2007.
[39]*Times-Courier* (Charleston) 31 August 2006.
[40]Sean Flanagan, "Ashmore," personal email (29 May 2009).
[41]Janice Tremeear, "Ashmore Estates," personal email (10 July 2009).
[42]Tyson Reed, "American Horrors," personal email (9 July 2009).

Bibliography

Allen, Howard W. and Vincent A. Lacey, eds. *Illinois Elections, 1818-1990: Candidates and County Returns for President, Governor, Senate, and House of Representatives*. Carbondale: Southern Illinois University Press, 1992.

Allen, John W. *Legends & Lore of Southern Illinois*. Carbondale: Southern Illinois University, 1963, 1973.

Allen-Kline, Margaret. "'She Protects Her Girls': The Legend of Mary Hawkins at Pemberton Hall." M.A. thesis, Eastern Illinois University, 1998.

Benjamin, Susan S. *Historic and Architectural Assessment: Charles A. Lindbergh School*. Chicago: Historic Certification Consultants, 1998.

Bielski, Ursula. *Chicago Haunts: Ghostlore of the Windy City*. Chicago: Lake Claremont Press, 1998.

Bielski, Ursula. *More Chicago Haunts: Scenes from Myth and Memory*. Chicago: Lake Claremont Press, 2000.

Brandon, Trent. *The Book of Ghosts*. Galloway: Zerotime Publishing, 2003.

Brooks, Rachel. *Chicago Ghosts*. Atglen: Schiffer Books, 2008.

Brunvand, Jan Harold. *The Vanishing Hitchhiker: American Urban Legends and Their Meanings*. New York: W.W. Norton & Company, 1981.

Brunvand, Jan Harold. *Too Good to be True: the Colossal Book of Urban Legends*. New York: W.W. Norton & Company, 1999, 2001.

Christensen, Jo-Anne. *Ghost Stories of Illinois*. Edmonton: Lone Pine, 2000.

Coleman, Charles H. *Eastern Illinois State College: Fifty Years of Public Service* in *Eastern Illinois State College Bulletin* 189 (January 1950).

Corliss, William R. *Handbook of Unusual Natural Phenomena: Eyewitness Accounts of Nature's Greatest Mysteries*. New York: Arlington House, 1986.

Crowe, Richard T. *Chicago's Street Guide to the Supernatural*. Oak Park: Carolando Press, 2000, 2001.

Franciscan Friars. National Catholic Camping Association. *St. Francis Boys Camp*. Libertyville: privately printed, 1961.

Gienapp, William E. *The Origins of the Republican Party, 1852-1856*. New York: Oxford University Press, 1987.

Graczyk, Jim and Donna Boonstra. *Field Guide to Illinois Hauntings*. Alton: Whitechapel Productions Press, 2001.

Gray, Wood. *The Hidden Civil War: The Story of the Copperheads*. New York: The Viking Press, 1942.

Guasco, Suzanne Cooper. "'The Deadly Influence of Negro Capitalists': Southern Yeomen and Resistance to the Expansion of Slavery in Illinois." *Civil War History* 47 (Winter 2001).

Harrelson, Ralph S. "History and Legend of Lakey." *Goshen Trails* (October 1973): 13.

Hauck, Dennis William. *Haunted Places: The National Directory: Ghostly Abodes, Sacred Sites, UFO Landings, and Other Supernatural Locations*. New York: Penguin Books, 1994, 1996.

Heise, Kenan. *Resurrection Mary: a Ghost Story*. Evanston: Chicago Historical Bookworks, 1990.

Johnson, Grant C. *Report of Coroner's Physician to the Coroner of Coles County, Illinois*. Springfield: Sangamon County Coroner's Office, 1980.

Kaczmarek, Dale. *Illuminating the Darkness: The Mystery of Spook Lights*. Oak Lawn: Ghost Research Society Press, 2003.

Kaczmarek, Dale. *Windy City Ghosts: An Essential Guide to the Haunted History of Chicago.* Oak Lawn: Ghost Research Society Press, 2000, 2005.

Kleen, Michael. *Legends and Lore of Illinois* 1 (March 2007): 1-6.

Kleen, Michael. *Legends and Lore of Illinois* 1 (August 2007): 1-6.

Kleen, Michael. "Interview with Kathi Kresol." *Legends and Lore of Illinois* 3 (June 2009): 6.

Lewis, Chad and Terry Fisk. *The Illinois Road Guide to Haunted Locations.* Eau Claire: Unexplained Research Publishing, 2007.

Markus, Scott. *Voices from the Chicago Grave: They're Calling. Will You Answer?* Holt: Thunder Bay Press, 2008.

McCarty, Michael and Connie Corcoran Wilson. *Ghostly Tales of Route 66: from Chicago to Oklahoma.* Wever: Quixote Press, 2008.

McCoy, Sarah J. Breese, et al. "Risk Factors for Postpartum Depression: A Retrospective Investigation at 4-Weeks Postnatal and a Review of the Literature." *The Journal of the American Osteopathic Association* 106 (April 2006): 193-198.

McKinney, Isabel. *Mr. Lord: The Life and Words of Livingston C. Lord.* Urbana: University of Illinois Press, 1937.

Neely, Charles, ed. *Tales and Songs of Southern Illinois.* Menasha: George Banta Publishing, 1938; reprint, Carbondale: Southern Illinois University Press, 1998.

Newton, Michael. *Savage Girls and Wild Boys: A History of Feral Children.* New York: Picador, 2004.

Nowlan, James D. "From Lincoln to Forgottonia." *Illinois Issues* 24 (September 1998): 27-30.

O'Malley, Suzanne. *Are You There Alone?: The Unspeakable Crime of Andrea Yates.* New York: Simon and Schuster, 2004.

Perry, Charles William. "Angeline Vernon Milner." *The Alumni Quarterly* 13 (May 1924): 2-10.

Rochefort, David A. *From Poorhouses to Homelessness: Policy Analysis and Mental Health Care.* Westport: Auburn House, 1997.

Rowe, Bill. "Was Byron's Barefoot Phantom Merely a Masquerade?" *Rockford Magazine* 11 (Fall 1996): 24-25.

Schwartz, Alvin. *Scary Stories Treasury: Three Books to Chill Your Bones.* Vol. 2, *More Scary Stories to Tell in the Dark.* New York: Harper Collins, 1984.

Scott, Beth and Michael Norman. *Haunted Heartland: True Ghost Stories from the American Midwest.* New York: Barnes & Noble Books, 1985, 1992.

Stanton, Carl L. *They Called it Treason: an Account of Renegades, Copperheads, Guerrillas, Bushwhackers and Outlaw Gangs that Terrorized Illinois During the Civil War.* Bunker Hill: by the author, 2002.

Taylor, Troy. *Haunted Decatur Revisited: Ghostly Tales from the Haunted Heartland of Illinois.* Alton: Whitechapel Productions Press, 2000.

Taylor, Troy. *Haunted Illinois: Travel Guide to the History and Hauntings of the Prairie State.* Alton: Whitechapel Productions Press, 2004.